The
Healing
Spirit

RIDER

THE
HEALING
SPIRIT

The Story of Dennis Barrett

Jack Angelo

RIDER

LONDON   SYDNEY   AUCKLAND   JOHANNESBURG

First published in 1990 by Rider
An imprint of Century Hutchinson Ltd
20 Vauxhall Bridge Road
London SW1V 2SA

Century Hutchinson Australia (Pty) Ltd
20 Alfred Street, Milsons Point, Sydney, NSW 2061,
Australia

Century Hutchinson New Zealand Ltd, PO Box 40-086,
32-34 View Road, Glenfield, Auckland 10, New Zealand

Century Hutchinson South Africa (Pty) Ltd,
PO Box 337, Bergvlei 2012, South Africa

Printed and bound by Mackays of Chatham

British Library Cataloguing in Publication Data
Angelo, Jack
  The healing spirit.
  1. Spiritual healing. Barrett, Dennis
  I. Title
  615.8'52'0924

ISBN 0-7126-3025-2

This book is dedicated to the spirit friends who have freely given their love, a small part of which is mentioned herein, and to the Source of that love.

Acknowledgements

To my wife, Jan, for her many ideas and suggestions, for her painstaking work in checking the manuscript at all stages, and for her constant support and encouragement. This book could not have been written without her.

To Oliver and Moyra Caldecott, who have set so much in motion.

To Marcia Cuff, for permission to reproduce her painting of Ho Yang Sen.

To Marion Peters, for permission to reproduce her photographs.

To Lucas Ralli, for permission to reproduce his photograph of the leaf apport.

To William Roepke, for permission to reproduce his verse and drawing.

To those who have allowed their names to be used.

To those who preferred their names to be changed for the sake of their privacy.

To all those who, over the years, have come to us for help and entrusted their health to Spirit.

Contents

Introduction

Lives are completely changed by disease and tragedy. Overnight, love and justice can become words without meaning. Yet those who deal with such events on a daily basis have to come to terms with them and somehow help the distressed to find purpose in their lives. This is the story of a healer, a man who has himself known personal tragedy, and who devotes his life to restoring the health of others, whether physical, mental, emotional or spiritual.

Dennis Barrett was born and brought up in Bristol where he still lives. His life seemed quite ordinary until his forties when he discovered his gift as a healer. The past twenty-five years have seen the development of this gift along with many other psychic abilities.

Dennis has never charged for his services though people are free to make donations, nor has he ever advertised; yet he is known to a grateful following worldwide. His patients have included many well-known people in the fields of medicine, entertainment, religion and politics (some of whom prefer not to be named in the text for personal reasons).

In 1985 Dennis suffered his second massive heart attack and came close to death, but this proved to be only the prelude to a busier and fuller life. After retiring from his job as a factory storekeeper he became a full-time healer and has travelled extensively in Britain and the USA as part of his work. Through Dennis, many serious illnesses have been cured and he has also been called in to help in cases of exorcism and haunting. As well as his private practice, he now gives regular healing demonstrations in South Wales and the West Country.

Dennis is a modest man of remarkable achievement. The spirit entities* who work with him call him 'a perfect instrument', meaning that he seeks nothing for himself and does his best to be as clear a channel as possible for the healing energies that he is able to attract (see Chapter Seven). 'People are interested in the message, not the colour of the telephone,' he says. This is probably true, but the range and quality of Dennis's abilities have been all-important in building the reputation he holds today.

During the writing of this book, he frequently went into trance so that his spirit helpers could come through. In this way, with Dennis's mediation, it has been possible to include their 'voices' and the information they wanted to pass on.

This book explains the complicated subject of spirit healing in simple, everyday language. Its scope is broad and the principles can be put into practice by anyone. From the thousands of cases which Dennis has dealt with, a number have been picked out in order to demonstrate the wide range of situations in which spirit healing can be helpful. The pressures of modern living often mean that people lose touch with their true selves and end up feeling unhealthy, unhappy and out of balance. Healing can help us rediscover our true selves, thus regaining the peace, joy and harmony which is every person's birthright.

Dennis tells his story in his own words, though here and there the 'voices' of his other inspirations can be detected, an approach which very much reflects the way he lives and works. Along with the case histories, Dennis's development as a healer emerges as an integral part of his growth as a person. His message is clearly one of comfort and upliftment, with an exciting future ahead for humanity.

The spirits have said that this book is their gift to Dennis

---

* In this book, *Spirit* is spelt with a capital letter when it signifies the God force. Where *spirit* signifies an adjective, as in the term 'spirit healing', or a particular spirit entity, a small letter is used.

to thank him for all he has done for others. Perhaps no further tribute is necessary.

ONE

The Corkscrew Baby

The man looked back at me as he turned to wave. A mixture of relief and quiet joy had replaced the strained expression I had seen an hour before. He hadn't known how to thank me. He stood there, open-mouthed, unable to speak. In a moment he was gone and the telephone was ringing back in my flat.

'Just like a normal Sunday,' I thought.

As I walked up the passage from the front door, I was mentally clearing my mind as, for a moment, the desperate look in his eyes still floated before me. I lifted the receiver. There was no time to say hello, or give my number.

'Mr Barrett, Mr Barrett! My baby, my baby!' The voice was hysterical. 'Oh, Mr Barrett, I . . .'

Her words broke up into choking sobs.

I recognized the voice and almost without thinking I saw myself put a reassuring arm around her.

'Yes,' I said, 'what about her?'

'She's all right – she's all right!' Again the voice rose to a shrill scream. 'She can roll over, the lump's gone!'

'But that's what you want, isn't it? What's all the noise about? It's what you said you wanted.'

My voice was calm, matter-of-fact, unruffled, but its off-hand tone shocked me since I am usually very sympathetic and conciliatory on the telephone. I was still playing the situation down as I continued: 'You're not surprised are you? You asked God for help, so why be surprised if he gives it to you?'

Her sobs began to subside. I recalled the night, just a

4

few days before, when I had first met her.

I had been taking a local Sunday service in Bristol as a medium. After the service, Betty Mills came up to me and asked if I would see her daughter since she had a baby of three months who was seriously ill. I agreed to see them the following week on a Thursday evening.

The daughter turned up with her husband.

'Mr Barrett? I'm Mrs Alloway, my mother made an appointment for us.'

They were a young couple. The baby, Jody, was well wrapped up and I couldn't see anything wrong with her. But her parents were so uptight and nervous, I was afraid to make any movement towards the child which might alarm them. It was obvious they were tense and didn't know what to expect and I was very aware of the fact that I had to be careful with them. So I sat by the side of the mother and asked if I could hold her.

It was like reaching for a cub in a lioness's den. She looked at me as if she might scratch my eyes out. The young man reassured her and gave her arm a squeeze.

'It's all right,' he whispered.

Her eyes flashed back at him and reluctantly she handed over the little bundle.

I held the child for about half a minute when she started to get irritable and began to wriggle. This was the sign I needed to hand her straight back to her mum. She clutched the baby tightly and soon the little body seemed at peace again.

I turned to the two of them. The husband had relaxed and settled back in his chair. 'Well, there we are,' I said, to break the silence.

Mrs Alloway swallowed hard. 'Don't you want to know what's the matter with her?'

'Not really,' I said. 'It's not important is it?'

She frowned. But before she could speak I continued: 'I'm not concerned with what was the matter with her before she came here. She's all right now, that's all I'm concerned about. I've done what I had to do.'

I could see that my words were making them a bit annoyed. Perhaps they were disappointed that I hadn't been aware of the baby's problem or noticed their own distress. But I knew that everything was all right because my spirit helpers had put the words in my mouth. I just let them come out. For some reason this was the approach that was needed.

The young man leaned forward. 'I'm sure we're grateful for whatever can be done for Jody, but I think you should know something about her. After she was born we wondered if something was wrong. First of all the hospital couldn't tell us. Then last month they took an x-ray which showed she had this complaint which contorts the spine, twists it slowly, like a corkscrew. Before she's nine months old, Jody's body will be bent in half. She'll never be able to sit up and she'll never walk.'

Tears began to fill Mrs Alloway's eyes. She didn't bother to brush them away, she just held on to the baby and let them roll down her cheeks. The young man put his arm round them both.

'Don't worry, love.' He looked down at his other hand. 'Jody's back is already twisting. According to the doctors, there's no way it can be stopped. We've just been told it's permanent and there's nothing they can do about it.'

In spite of their obvious anxiety, I felt a peace around us. For a few moments we sat together in silence.

Mrs Alloway blinked back her tears. 'They've made an appointment for Jody to see a specialist tomorrow. What do we do now? You say she'll get better.'

'Just go and see him and take it as it comes,' I said. 'Don't worry about anything. Just go through the motions. Let me know what happens if you like.'

The couple were still mystified as they left, but a good deal of the tension had disappeared. They thanked me and promised to let me know if there was any change in the situation.

After they had gone I washed my hands. This is something I always do since it mentally clears away the condition I have just been involved with. I can then forget all about it and feel free to tackle the next problem.

The following day they saw the specialist and he was horrified at how badly the child was already deformed.

There was no apparent improvement. He told the couple that Jody had infantile scoliosis and there wasn't much that could be done for her, but they would try to alleviate things in the meantime.

'Physiotherapy is all we can offer, I'm afraid. Would you be agreeable to that?'

The couple said they would agree to anything which would help their baby and he called the physiotherapy department and asked them to do what they could to fit her in for an urgent appointment. The appointment was made for the following Wednesday.

Mike Alloway got up early on Sunday morning to go to work. As usual he went to look in on Jody. He paused at the doorway. There was something different about the room. Jody was sleeping peacefully in her cot but the atmosphere had changed in some way. He decided not to enter the room.

It was some time later when Jody's mother was getting her ready for her bath. She laid the child down and turned to get the soap. In that moment, Jody rolled over on to her stomach, a thing she had never been able to do before. Something about her had definitely changed.

Jackie Alloway's hands shook as she began to undress the little girl. Finally the last garment fell away to reveal a perfect body. She grabbed the child in disbelief, running her hands over the previously deformed spine. Emotion surged through her.

'Oh, God, I don't believe it! It's true, it's true. What's happened, Jody?'

A smile from the baby said it all.

The next moment she was on the phone to me. When she had got over her hysteria she told me what had happened. She told me about the visit to the specialist and the physiotherapy appointment for the following Wednesday.

'What shall I do, Mr Barrett?'

'Go through with it and see how it works out.'

'But she's all right!'

'Never mind that. Go and keep the appointment anyway.'

She calmed down and rang off and a few days later she

7

called again to tell me the rest of the story.

She and Jody went to the clinic with Mike and Jody's grandmother, Betty Mills. They sat in the waiting room and the physiotherapist came out and looked around and went back in again. The time for the appointment came and went. The physiotherapist was still coming out and looking around and going back in again. After a while she turned to Jody's mother.

'I've been expecting a woman with a little baby as an emergency case. She ought to have been here half an hour ago and she hasn't turned up. You haven't seen anyone like that looking in, have you?'

'My appointment was for half an hour ago. This is Jody and I'm her mother.'

The physiotherapist took a good look at Jody. 'Oh, no. There must be some mistake. You can't be.'

Jackie Alloway showed her the card. 'Well this is the baby and I'm Mrs Alloway her mother.'

'But your baby hasn't got infantile scoliosis. Never in this world!'

Mike and Jackie found it difficult to hold back the tears and soon Nanny was crying tears of joy and relief with them. Then, to everyone's amazement, Jody began to giggle loudly.

The physiotherapist telephoned the specialist to confirm the situation. He said he would see them the next day to check it himself. But when he examined Jody he was as puzzled as the physiotherapist. 'Hmm. I could say this isn't the same baby since she no longer appears to have the condition she had last Friday . . .'

X-rays were taken which showed that this was the case. Later, slides of the x-rays, taken before the healing and after, were presented to the Alloways by the hospital (see photo insert).

That was in 1984, and Jody has grown up to be a perfect little madam in every respect. People still come to see me and say 'Jody's mother sent me.'

Since 1984 life has grown for me too, becoming richer and fuller. Now I expect the unexpected. But I have often pondered over how it all came to pass, how all the adventures I have had could have happened to me. If someone had told me twenty-five years ago that I would become a healer and clairvoyant medium, I would have laughed in their face and told them not to be so stupid. I didn't have time for all that rubbish. I thought it was rubbish then. Spirits were either something in a bottle or what doolally old ladies went on about; certainly not the total reality I know them to be now.

So when did I change my mind? What drove me on cold winter evenings, all those years ago, to sit at the back of Spiritualist meetings just to keep warm? I used to catch myself chuckling as I walked down Broadmead thinking, what will a man do just to keep warm! If I hadn't felt so lonely then, so desperate and unhappy, would any of it have happened? I know better now. I know that we all have a part to play in life and that sooner or later we must play it. There are forces which point us in the right direction and it is up to us whether we take it. Tragedy, illness, pain, or something wonderful like a chance meeting, hearing the right words spoken at the right time, the look in someone's eyes . . . whatever it is, something urges us on to play the part we came to play.

It was just before Christmas 1965. My marriage had broken up and we had decided to separate. It was one of the most painful times in my life. Suddenly I had to say goodbye to my wife, my children and my home. All I could afford at the time was a tiny bedsitting room. It had a gas stove and a one-bar electric fire which the landlady didn't want me to put on unless I was in the room. So if I left the room to go to the toilet, I'd often come back to find it switched off!

I was so lonely and miserable, I just wandered round the streets of Bristol. Occasionally there was enough money left to have a drink in a pub. There I heard somebody talking about Spiritualist churches. They were dotted all round Bristol then and there was one open every day of the week. You couldn't go into a club unless you were a member, but you could go into a Spiritualist church whenever the door was open.

I soon found out the truth of this. They were warm and comfortable and a better alternative to sitting in that bleak little room. People smiled at me, but they left me alone. Sometimes I would strike up a conversation, but no one tried to pry.

At first I just sat there when their meetings started, grateful for a bit of comfort and the sound of human voices. Then, as I began to pay more attention, I realized that something seemed familiar. I had been to a Spiritualist church before, in 1949, but I had put the event right out of my mind. I hadn't been married long and I was young and impressionable. One of my aunts was attending a church regularly then. She had a soft spot for me and she would take me on one side and tell me stories about what she had heard and what she had seen. But I thought she was crazy. She insisted that it was possible to 'see' and 'hear' with other senses and that these 'psychic senses', as she called them, were the gateway to the wonderful world of Spirit which the majority of us were missing.

I am a sceptical sort of person and I need proof before I will accept anything. Belief has never been enough for me, it has to be something built on my own experience. I shared these conversations with my wife and we decided to investigate and find out for ourselves what my aunt was so enthusiastic about. After all, the churches were filled with other people apart from my aunt. They couldn't all be mad.

So one night the three of us went up there together. It turned out to be quite an experience. The building was like a little chapel inside. At the far end was a platform on which two elderly women sat behind a table. They each had a glass of water in front of them. The only other things on the table were a vase of flowers, a note pad and a Bible. People were sitting talking to each other quite normally and everybody seemed to know everyone else.

My aunt nudged me and whispered: 'We've a wonderful medium here tonight, Dennis. Maybe you'll get a message.'

The thought of some disembodied voice whispering in my other ear put the wind up me straight away and I prepared for the worst. Suddenly the room went quiet and one of the ladies behind the table stood up. 'Good evening, friends,' she said and beamed at everyone.

The congregation said 'Good evening' back. She then went on to say that she was delighted to welcome the speaker for the night who was a well-known and well-loved medium. She sat down again and a hymn was sung with great gusto. I was fond of singing and I soon found myself relaxing and joining in.

I can't remember the name of the medium that night, but I do remember her presence. Although she was short she seemed to fill the end of the hall. She spoke slowly with a surprisingly clear, firm voice. I can't remember what she talked about, but I do remember the kindliness in her voice and the fact that she did not use any notes. When she had finished talking we sang another hymn. Soon the first lady, who seemed to be chairing the service, announced that it was time for clairvoyance and that our guest speaker was going to give it.

All eyes turned to the medium. She was sitting quietly with her eyes closed. A moment later she stood up and took a step forward, looking to one side of the congregation. She pointed at someone and said: 'I have to come to you, my dear. I have an old lady with me and she says she wishes to speak to you.'

She then went on to describe the 'old lady' who was 'with her' in some detail and asked if the person in the congregation could place her.

'Yes,' she said, she certainly could, it was her mother.

'I'm so glad you said that,' said the medium, 'because she brings such a lot of love with her and I feel . . .'

I sat there in a daze. The medium went from person to person talking about people she said she could 'see'. They took her into homes and she could describe the furniture and the decorations with ease. It was all some kind of proof for those in the congregation, proof that it really was mother or some dead friend who had turned up to communicate with us in that little church. I felt light-headed. The sceptical part of me wanted an answer.

Then my aunt was nudging me again. 'Den!' she hissed.

'She's talking to you. Give her an answer!'

I looked up. The medium was staring straight at me. She smiled. 'Can I have your voice, dear? I need to hear your voice to make the link.'

'Oh, yes,' I croaked.

She then outlined events that had happened in my life and told me things about myself that even my wife didn't know about. This was to give me proof that the person from the world of Spirit who was there with her really knew me well. But I still felt she knew more about me than I thought she ought to. My aunt did her best to explain that it was to prove the survival of the human spirit, but the whole experience frightened me to death. I didn't go there again!

And now I was back in a Spiritualist church, thinking how clever I was in finding a place to keep warm. Things were very much the same, I noticed. The same hymns were being sung. Most of the congregation were elderly women. But I was looking at them afresh. I began to wonder if my new-found place of refuge would get me involved in something I neither understood nor wanted in my life – a life that was traumatic enough already.

Nobody could make me do anything against my will, I decided. It would be my choice if anything happened. So I would continue using the few churches I had selected as places of sanctuary as long as I needed them. Besides, they were homely places where, I realized with surprise, I felt at peace.

One evening I set off for the Bedminster church. I turned my coat collar up against the cold wind and mused about the medium who was billed as the visiting speaker. I had my head down as I came through the door, but the first person who saw me recognized me straight away. It was Billy Thomas. His Welsh voice was unmistakable. 'Hello, Dennis. You're a healer, then.'

I was flabbergasted. I had last seen him when I was a fireman on the Great Western Railway during the war. He didn't have time to say much more and ushered me to a seat. 'I'll see you later, Den. We've a lot to talk about.'

I sat in the pew with my heart thumping. Of all the people to bump into. We had been good friends, but I didn't know he was a Spiritualist. I had never heard the word 'healer' before. I had never heard of healing. I had been so busy going to work, working overtime and coming home and going to bed, I don't think I even read the paper. What did he mean? I dismissed the remark. It was the sort of daft thing my aunt might have said.

Most of the service passed me by, I was too busy with my own thoughts. I remembered Billy Thomas as a good railway man, down-to-earth, level-headed and with a great sense of humour, not the sort to get mixed up with 'seeing' and 'hearing'. And now he was talking about 'healing'. I would slip away at the end of the service. It meant that I would have to cross this church off my list now that I had met Billy again.

But when the service ended there was no escape. My seat was in the middle of the row and Billy was coming towards me with the medium. He beckoned me to come and meet her. 'This is a very old friend, Dennis.'

She looked me straight in the eye and gripped my hand gently but firmly. She smiled warmly. Billy looked from one of us to the other. 'Well, what do you think, then?'

'Oh, yes,' she said, 'he's a healer, isn't he?'

So that was two with the same opinion within an hour. I came away thinking they were a little bit touched, but I would still go back to the church and see what others had to say. I needed an explanation of why they thought I was a healer and I was curious as to what this might mean.

Over the following weeks, various mediums gave me a 'message' which always included the fact that I was a healer and that I should 'get on with it!' Some of them would talk to me after the service about it and I became convinced that they were sincere in their belief that I could heal the sick, even though I doubted it myself.

One night, a woman kindly offered to run me home. I didn't have far to go, but she insisted on giving me a lift. As soon as we were both seated in the car she turned to me and said: 'As you're a healer, will you do something about my back?'

'Don't be daft,' I replied. 'I don't know what to do, I've never seen healing done. I don't know what they're talking about anyway.'

'Well,' she said, 'they all say you're a healer. Come on and do something about it.'

I began to feel embarrassed, hoping it was not some kind of proposition. 'I'd rather not.'

'Oh, come on, Dennis. I only want you to touch my back. It won't take a moment. What have you got to lose?'

'Look, I thought you wanted to give me a lift home,' I said. 'I can get out and walk if you like.'

She started the car and we drove to the street where I was staying. All the while she kept insisting that now was my chance to prove I was a healer. The car had stopped and she was still pleading in this way so, to pacify her, just as I was getting out of the car I leaned over and put my hand between the seat and her back. As I touched her spine, it was as if something went 'click' inside me.

'Oh,' she groaned, 'that's it!'

'Shut up,' I said, 'and mind your own business!'

My rudeness only encouraged her. 'But that's where it is.'

'I know. Just keep quiet!'

I kept my hand there for about three minutes. When I took it away she was gasping for breath. 'It's gone. You've done it!'

I said goodnight quickly and dashed indoors. I was actually glad to see the one-bar fire again. I looked out of the window to the street below. The car hadn't moved. As I drew the curtains I found my hands were shaking with excitement. I wanted to laugh out loud. The woman had not been putting me on. I *had* felt something in my hands. I knew exactly where to put them and I also knew afterwards that her back condition had been healed. Was this what they meant by 'healer'? I was still sceptical. It would take more than one incident like that to convince me.

The following week I was talking to a man after the service. He was clutching his head and complaining about a headache.

'What's wrong?' I asked him.

'I've got this terrible migraine,' he said. 'I used to hope that it would go by coming here, but it just seems to get worse.'

I had always understood until then that migraine headaches were a serious condition which you just had to put up with and I asked him if this was so.

'I don't know. I just wish to God somebody could do something about it.'

I found myself saying: 'That's the right bloke to wish to. You can call it a prayer if you like, it's just the same.'

As I said this I was thinking, What am I talking about?

Then he went quiet and said: 'What are you doing?'

I hadn't put my hands anywhere near him, but he was aware of something. 'Just be quiet a minute,' I said quickly. I felt the moment pass, as if something had been completed and I started to talk about something else.

He was shaking his head and smiling. 'I'm not disagreeing with you. The pain has completely gone.'

The knowledge that I could help others began to dawn and it felt good. I still doubted my abilities, not realizing that I was doubting the abilities of those in Spirit who were working through me. I needed immediate answers to all the hundreds of questions that were bubbling up inside me.

Billy Thomas sensed this and was always willing to give up his time to clear away my doubts. As a medium he sometimes used Tarot cards and one night he gave me a reading.

'Den, you're a lucky man. You've got it all to come. You don't know the half of what's in front of you. You'll be travelling far. You'll be doing all sorts of things and you'll be doing things that nobody dreamed were possible.'

'I find it difficult to accept all this, Billy,' I said.

'Maybe. But I was right about the healing, wasn't I? Just bide your time, you'll see. They'll lead you to it. You'll be dealing with all aspects of psychic work too, not just healing. But healing will be your main work and so many good things in life will come out of it.'

What he was describing was unbelievable. Here I was with my life in ruins and he was painting this picture of a glorious future I couldn't begin to imagine. But Billy wasn't making a cruel joke. 'I know you can't see it now, Dennis, but this is what they're telling me. You can trust them. I have and they've never let me down yet. You can hold your head high. You're on your way, boy!'

I laughed nervously. 'What is happening to me, Billy?'

He ignored my question. 'You're not the sort of person who can be encouraged to sit down and spend years and years training for something. In your case you don't need any training. You have one vital ingredient. You have love in your heart, Den. If you have love in your heart, healing must follow. Love is the motivating force. It's the expression of energy between any two God forces – a man and a woman, a patient and a healer . . . You cannot help people unless you love them. You cannot help people if you have no respect for them. You cannot help people whom you despise and you cannot help people if you are looking to see what you can get out of it. When you are healing or giving clairvoyance or anything like that, your first responsibility is to yourself, to be honest and not grasping.'

He paused and shook his head, smiling. 'But I don't need to tell you all this. You know it already, it's part of you, Den.'

I was stunned by what he was saying and yet at the same time I knew that it was what I could have told him. I have found that so many who make a business out of spiritual work find it difficult to tune in to Spirit because their minds are working like calculators, wondering if they have the time to do this or get away with that before the next patient comes. In effect they have put the barriers up; barriers that stop their spirit helpers from working, barriers that stop their patients from getting full benefit. In healing one has to be whole-hearted and one has to feel love for the patient.

That conversation took place twenty years ago. Looking back, it seems to me as if Spirit were pulling out all the stops to impress me, to convince me that I had the gift of healing. It was for me to believe it and get on and use it, and I did.

Billy was right. As a result of what he said I have accepted every challenge that has come along and the challenges have been tremendous. I have never said no to anything, whether it has been clearing houses of unwanted spirit friends or dealing with people who thought they were possessed, or taking trips abroad in response to calls for help because I felt that inspiration was telling me it was right to do so. I have never said no to any challenge, mainly because Billy said it would work and the spirits would never let me down. And they never have.

Every time I see him and tell him what I have been doing, he chuckles and says: 'I told you so!'

TWO

A Healer in the Making

When you have been down for some time you tend to see the world in a negative way. Such is the power of the mind, our moods can affect every person and every situation we come into contact with. After the break-up of my marriage I felt worthless and of no use to anyone. The one thing that might have made me feel better was the chance to help others. But there was little chance of that at work, or so I thought then.

I was trying not to go under, trying not to isolate myself, and my visits to Spiritualist churches were an attempt to stay in contact with others. I was looking for something, but I did not know what it was. I just needed someone to believe in me again and then I might start believing in myself.

I had the will to reconstruct my life, but my emotions constantly let me down. I felt bad about myself. I worried about my family. Other people's tragedies and problems affected me and so did the disastrous events that regularly occurred in the world at large. People sometimes noticed this and shook their heads sadly. 'Den, you take things too seriously. You're too sensitive.'

That was when I had been off my guard and lowered the barriers. But I had made myself a thick skin in order to cope, and I had started creating this layer of protection around myself long before, in childhood, when I found out how easily others could hurt me if I let them.

Being sensitive means that you will always be aware of the sufferings of others and sympathize with them and this is essential for a healer. But it is also essential to learn how to live with sensitivity and to control your own reactions; otherwise you can be destroyed by your own feelings and the hard knocks that life has to give. In my early life I couldn't come to terms with my deepest feelings so I buried them and made sure others didn't know about them.

To understand the part that my feelings have played in fashioning my life, I have had to think about my family and the way I grew up within it. Undoubtedly those who are capable of feeling compassion for others are born with this quality but I am sure that it can be reinforced by one's upbringing.

My mother always seemed a gentlewoman and she brought me up to be gentle in nature. 'You've got four sisters,' she would say. 'Treat every woman as if she is your sister.'

The story goes that her family came from a country estate up near Gloucester, called Longney, near the River Severn. Generations ago, the youngest son ran off with a serving maid and they came down the Severn on a barge to Bristol. They got off at Bristol docks and soon found themselves a little cottage near the dockside. The girl used to make her own bread because this had been one of her tasks in the manor house. She put it out to cool on the windowsill and passersby often asked if she could spare them a loaf. This gave them the idea of turning the cottage into a bakery. The business thrived and they built their own bakehouse. My grandfather became a master baker and was later elected president of the Master Bakers Association of Great Britain.

The same courtesy and respect for others which had been practised at the estate became part of family life in the home of the two runaways. This was passed down through the generations and I was always aware of my mother's high moral standards, which even then seemed above the norm. She had an answer for everything, but it was never a rude or rough answer, always a gentle response.

She had a habit of quoting poetry or an old saying whenever there was a point that needed making. 'A stitch in time saves nine' was one of her favourites.

If I was putting off a job that needed doing she would say: 'You don't want to do it?'

'No.'

'Why not?'

'It'll take too long to do it.'

'It'll take a lot longer tomorrow because it'll be a lot more to do. Do it now, Dennis.'

I used to say 'Oh, all right!' and go away feeling ratty because she had proved again that she was right. But her kindly approach could overcome my stubbornness and I realize what a big influence she had in forming my character. Since she died I have found her attitudes reflected in my own responses to situations and I have been told by mediums that they have seen her working through me.

There was a loving atmosphere in the home which made it happy and peaceful. We had our rows, our differences, but the way we resolved these seemed to bind us together. My three sisters slept in one room. My brother and I slept in another room and my baby sister slept in mother's room for a time. When my eldest sister left home, my youngest sister moved in with the other two girls. This was the way it worked. We were a close-knit family and God help the one who tried to snipe at any one of us.

Our ideals and expectations were high and in many ways I must have seemed a bit prim and proper to my friends. I also used to be very easily upset. This wasn't considered unusual at home, but as I ventured out into the world I found that not everybody was as soft and sentimental. Had I been in a different situation then, I would probably have made an extremely good sensitive at quite an early age.

But the realities of life at elementary school soon taught me to be a bit more practical. If I ever expressed sentiment or emotion I was scorned or laughed at. There were many who could not accept even an arm around the shoulders. I had to learn to harden myself so that I didn't get hurt and so that I didn't react emotionally to other people's insensitivity.

I was quite used to defending myself and fighting for my own opinions, even if this meant using my fists, and I soon realized I had a good 'right hook'. To be honest, I often enjoyed a good fight because it would clear the air and get rid of the adrenalin that had built up during a verbal argument. There were unwritten rules which we all accepted. It was as if we understood that there had to be a safety valve to let off steam. But that was all. We didn't need to hurt each other badly to feel satisfied.

Gang warfare was another outlet for our tensions that later cooled our tempers. The battlefield would be set up at night on an old building site. We would get our trenches ready and procure galvanized-iron sheets and planks of wood. Behind these a store of stones and broken bricks was laid up. Between us was a no man's land which no one could cross. When everything looked satisfactory, we would call out to the other gang: 'Are you ready?'

If the answer was yes, we would fling a barrage of stones at each other. Soon the air became thick with dust and curses as stones hit iron sheets. Eventually there would be a shout and a handkerchief waved. 'Call a truce. Charlie've bin 'urt!'

A bit of blood on your opponent was all you needed to feel that honour had been satisfied and once we were well tired out we would call it a day and go off together the best of pals. I never saw anybody being really aggressive. We just had a fight and that was it.

My parents weren't religious in the accepted sense. Mum and Dad didn't practise anything. Mother was too busy looking after the family to have any time left for church. There were six children to care for and she did all her own washing. I can remember her starting the washing at six in the morning and she would still be ironing at ten o'clock at night.

Sometimes Dad would walk to work in Avonmouth to save the fare because I needed a pair of shoes. When I did get a new pair of shoes, I would immediately climb a wall and scuff the newness out of them. The same would happen with a new pair of trousers, the newness had to be rubbed out of them. It was not a good thing to stand out among the rest of the boys and even worth a telling-off at home.

But the attitude which our parents had towards us and each other instilled in us the kind of loving feelings which I would call religious. This atmosphere of love permeated everything and generated a sense of peace and happiness. I think a happy atmosphere is a spiritual atmosphere in itself.

My older brother's favourite pastime was to lose himself in a book. Once he had read a book he could tell you everything about it. He would read a book from cover to cover, put it down and pick up another and read that. If there was anything left over from tea, mother would put it by the side of him as he read. Absent-mindedly he would munch away as he turned the pages. I have known him to eat a full plate of bread and butter, some dozen slices, after he had just finished eating a big tea. Then he would mark his place, look up and say: 'What's for supper Mum?'

Unlike Ronald, I found reading a chore, though I loved being read to. This made it difficult for me at school and I found book-learning hard going. Ronald could create his own world from a book but I looked out to the world of experience and any little jobs I could do were a welcome relief from lessons. I worked first thing in the morning, before school started, during the dinner hour and again in the evening after tea. I had a newspaper round and a job cleaning at the picture house on Saturdays.

This all brought in a nice bit of pocket money and I earned more while I was at school than I did when I started work at the age of fourteen. I put as much as I could into a Post Office savings account.

My sisters loved to spoil me and allowed me to get away with murder. Edna was always short of money after the weekend and I used to count out my savings in front of her and say: 'Don't you want to borrow any money, Edna?' She used to borrow three and sixpence on a Monday and give me back three and ninepence on a Friday. I had charged her threepence interest!

The front room of our house was reserved for visitors and important callers. It was also the courting room. If the boyfriend came round to see my eldest sister Olive on a Sunday afternoon, I would go and sit in with them until they had given me some money to go away and buy sweets. So I was quite a wide boy. I had all the makings of a businessman then, but this aptitude for making money deserted me in later life.

Apart from the valve radio, which needed constant nursing, we made all our own entertainment. We spent most of the time we had together talking among ourselves. When visitors came round, the piano provided our favourite diversion. Dad would take his seat and everyone gathered round for a singsong. He played well. My mother used to say he could get a tune out of any instrument, even if he had never seen it before.

Where my mother was the genteel philosopher in the family, my father was the great debater. He was a down-to-earth, practical and very matter-of-fact man. He didn't have the benefit of a good education, but he always used his common sense and intellect to analyse things. He would look things up and find out about them. If it was to do with politics, religion or some philosophical point, he would deliberately investigate both sides of the case so that he could discuss it from either point of view.

This made him very knowledgeable and it is an attitude he passed on to me. He could put his opinion over in a very forceful manner, but it was always laced with his wonderful sense of humour. I realized quite early in life how humour prevented one from becoming pompous or pretentious and how it could defuse a tense situation by helping people to relax and see the funny side of things.

There was nothing he liked better than a good discussion and he encouraged me to debate questions with him. He explained that it wasn't because he had to win a point or because he held a certain view, but for the sheer delight in the mental exercise. He would have gone down well with the ancient Greeks, for he had really mastered the art of involving someone in debate, and I usually found

23

myself in the middle of one before I knew it. If, for example, I said something in favour of the Labour Party, he would argue against it just to sharpen my wits. Another time he would argue against Conservative policies; again, to show me how blinkered we can become by sticking to a belief without thinking about it deeply. In later years I came to understand how much he taught me by playing the devil's advocate.

One evening, the young minister from the local Baptist chapel called. My brother and I were both working at the time and had not been home long. Dad went to answer the door. The minister looked past him and saw the two of us sitting at the table. 'Good evening,' said the minister. 'I've just taken over the Baptist chapel at the top of your street. I was wondering if you would like to send your two boys to our Bible class.'

'No, I would not,' said Dad. 'We don't do things like that here. They're big enough lads to please themselves. If they want to go to Bible class, they'll go, I won't have to send them.'

'I understand,' said the minister, a little taken aback. 'Well how about you all coming along to chapel to help build up the congregation a bit more? We've already got a good number and you would all be very welcome.'

'All right,' said Dad. 'We'll be up on a Sunday evening. You can expect us.'

'Thank you so much.' The minister shook his hand and left pretty quickly. He probably couldn't believe his luck.

So the next Sunday, Dad kept his word and we put in an appearance up in the gallery of the chapel, overlooking the pulpit. I was enjoying it. I could see that the minister was very nervous, but he got through his service somehow. At the end of the service, we went downstairs to make our way out. The minister was waiting to shake hands with us all.

'I'm so glad you came,' he said, smiling at Dad.

'I'm never coming again!'

Dad's reaction shocked the minister. 'Why not?' he asked.

'Because I've heard nothing that I couldn't have learned if I'd read the same book as you have read. When you learn to speak from your heart, I'll want to listen!'

And with that he wished the minister a very good night and we went home.

Again, my father was true to his word and he didn't return. I continued to go, and several weeks later he asked me how the young man had shaped up.

I told the truth. 'He's improving,' I said. 'He's interesting.'

'Right. I'll come again, then.'

He came the following Sunday and sat in the same place in the gallery. The minister noticed him and I could see he was surprised. When we came down the stairs at the end of the service, he left the people he was talking to and came over to Dad.

'I'm glad to see you again, Mr Barrett.'

'I'm glad I came. It was worth listening to.'

The minister's smile spread from ear to ear. If he had been given a thousand pounds I don't think he would have appreciated it more than these words of praise from a man who was fair and honest in his judgements.

That was the kind of lesson I learned from Dad and it was the way I was brought up. I was taught from quite young that it is never wise to prevaricate or to resort to flattery. If you can't be straight then you should hold your peace. I sometimes found this to be a handicap when I was younger. It didn't always pay to be honest. But I came to see that it benefits both you and those you are talking to because they know where they stand. It also made me realize that if you don't want a particular answer it is best not to ask the question.

I put this into practice when we were due to attend a wedding. People were trying on their outfits and a woman came up to me, dressed in what she considered to be the height of fashion. She wanted my opinion about it. 'How do you like my new hat?' she asked and turned around like a bird preening its feathers.

I didn't like it and I told her so. She looked horrified and walked away. Somebody asked me why I had spoken to her like that. 'I gave her my honest opinion,' I said.

Later she appeared with a different hat which looked a lot better. Some of the guests were going up to her and complimenting her. I would have felt awful if I had said 'That's lovely' just to please her, while everybody else tittered behind her back. I had behaved just like my father would have done and it was right for me too.

When Dad was courting my mother, her father taught him to be a baker and started him off with a bakehouse of his own in Hot Wells, not far from the original one. He worked day and night. The baking started around three or four in the morning so that the bread was always fresh. Then, during the day, he would go off and do an insurance round.

When the 1914-1918 war started, he joined the army before he needed to and left mother to run the bakehouse with a few workmen. But without my father she was unable to continue the business successfully and by the end of the war she was obliged to close it down.

Almost as soon as he arrived in Europe, Dad was captured and put in a prisoner-of-war camp. One day some German officers came round in the early hours of the morning asking for a few volunteers. Dad was quick to step out. He did this because he hadn't been a prisoner for long and knew he was fitter than most.

They took him off in a cart and he ended up in a German bakehouse with four other men. Even though he was only five foot three, he was detailed to carry two-hundred-weight sacks of flour up a flight of stone steps into the loft to store them. They unloaded nearly five tons of flour from the cart and stacked them up in the loft. When they had finished, the guard ordered them back to the prison camp. The baker overheard the order and refused to let them go. 'No,' he said. 'These men have worked hard. They are going to stay here and have their breakfast.'

The baker was a friendly man and soon they were trying to communicate with each other. Dad didn't speak a word of German, but the baker was doing his best to understand him. During the 'conversation' Dad told him he was a baker too. The German was delighted and soon arranged for him to be attached to the bakehouse. He was so good at pastry that he spent the rest of the war doing this while the German made the bread.

My father came away from the war with a good impression of the Germans. He said that, like most people, they were all right if they were treated with respect. He had many experiences during those years which we loved to hear about as we all sat round together. There was one sergeant in the camp who used to chain-smoke cigarettes. He never took more than a few puffs before he threw them away. Everywhere he went he was dropping lighted cigarettes in front of the prisoners so that they could have one. He went on doing this round the camp for as long as Dad could remember. This intrigued him because most of the soldiers had a brutal, brusque front which made them very aggressive. One day the sergeant noticed my father looking at him and came up to him. 'I know what you have been wondering, my friend. I am a father and my son is a prisoner of war in England. When you write home, please tell them we are not all bad.'

These sorts of stories made us think. We could picture the sergeant as a human being just like our dad.

He studied our faces carefully. 'The principle is, don't treat anybody with less than respect.'

Mother's teaching was the same, especially where girls were concerned. Every girl was somebody's daughter, perhaps somebody's sister and you had to treat them accordingly. I knew that all right and the principle seemed to work fine until I began to go out with them.

I had turned fifteen and this particular young girl wanted to break off our friendship. I was baffled by her response and asked her what was the matter.

'You're too slow,' she said. And I knew she didn't want to bother with me any more.

Mother's principles seemed to have let me down. I went home quite angry about this and Mother was quick to notice my mood.

'What's wrong, Den? Have you lost a shilling and found sixpence?'

I told her what had happened with my girlfriend and she listened carefully. 'It's all right for you to talk about sisters and daughters, but what about her? She said I was too slow.'

Mother nodded. 'Well, Den, you're old enough to learn something else now. You treat every woman as if she's a lady when you're in public and there are other people about, and you treat that woman as if she's the only woman in the world when you're on your own with her.'

My first wife was pure and truthful in everything she did, but she was exceedingly modest. I respected this even when I had to nurse her during the few occasions when she was ill. At such times I think my healing qualities were coming through because she said that just my being around her made her feel better. I used to wonder if these were the first signs of healing, but now I look further back for other clues.

It was a relief to say goodbye to school at the age of fourteen, but in the outside world anxiety was building up as Europe witnessed the effects of Hitler's rise to power. That year we heard Neville Chamberlain's broadcast on the radio – Great Britain was now at war with Germany. Dad had seen it coming and said there was a new breed of German he hadn't encountered in the First World War. Many opinions were expressed in our house and there was a sense of foreboding about the future. Mother said the women in the shops were talking about food rationing and we had better get ready for the bombs. I couldn't imagine what this meant, but everyone in Bristol was soon to find out.

As a teenager I was more impressed by the excitement that the war brought. We used to go up on the roof of the engraving works where I was an office boy to watch the dogfights, rather than go down to the bomb shelter. A night raid was the most exciting of all. The air would be filled with the sound of aircraft, gunfire, sirens wailing and bells ringing. Searchlights swept the dark skies which already glowed with buildings on fire. It was like a gigantic firework display, in which, during the next few years, large parts of the city were destroyed.

After three jobs as a general dogsbody, I was lucky to be taken on by the Great Western Railway. I was sixteen, I needed plenty of hard work to occupy me and I got it. The war years made working hours erratic and sometimes very long. In 1942 I tried to join the army, but railway work was designated a reserved occupation. Young firemen were lucky if they worked with a friendly driver, but if this happened real comradeship could develop. When I did come across expressions of kindness they were usually hidden behind a gruff facade of manly toughness.

While I was working on the railway, I heard about the St John Ambulance Brigade. If you were willing to join and learn first aid, there were a few shillings a year in it for anyone who had the qualification. The thought of a bit more money and something to do in my spare time was attractive, so I joined the Brigade and became a first aid man. It was a time when any knowledge of first aid was urgently needed.

I had found an outlet for my healing energies and I was being drawn towards the work, although I didn't realize this at the time. So I trace the beginnings of practical service back to these teenage years. I learned about anatomy and how to cope with an injured body, from a slight accident to a serious emergency. I enjoyed being a first aider for it got me out and about and involved in all sorts of situations.

By the time the war ended, various experiences of backstabbing had left me disillusioned with the railway and with many men whom I had considered friends rather than mere workmates. I sought to get my release, but this was not possible until the abolition of labour control in 1946.

I had 'the key of the door' and it was not long before I got a job in Capper Pass's scrap metal factory in Bedminster, where I worked with the storekeeper, Bill Brine. I soon found that Bill was a sensitive man and we became good friends. He used to look after the works football team. If any of the team had bruises they would see Bill as soon as they could and he would treat them. They said he had magic hands. This, coupled with his knowledge and sympathetic feelings, made him a true healer. He could instinctively tell whether anybody had a serious injury or not. If he saw someone and said 'That's a hospital job', nobody argued – he was always right.

My St John Ambulance work had stood me in good stead and I started carrying out first aid in the works. Eventually I was allowed to carry the little black bag and the magic sponge at football meetings. I was developing this side of my personality more and more and it became a lifeline to me in countering the effects of the monotonous work in the factory.

Bill Brine also encouraged me to join the ambulance service. In Bristol we have what is called the Bristol City and Marine Ambulance Corps. This was started at the turn of the century by a sea captain who wanted to do something about the lack of medical facilities at the dockside. He used to arrange for patients to be collected on a stretcher and conveyed to hospitals on a cart. That was the only form of 'ambulance' that was available when he started. The captain used to cart people himself over the dockside cobblestones to the nearby General Hospital. By the time I joined, of course, they had motorized ambulances.

We used to attend motor racing meetings at Castle Combe. On one such occasion the morning had begun with a downpour of rain which kept up for most of the day. We were stationed at different parts of the course and the ambulance was parked by the medical tents. There was a practice going on in the morning. 500 cc cars with open cockpits were racing round. The driver in the lead skidded on a corner and lost his grip on the track. The car veered over to the left, hit the grass bank and ricocheted right across the track. We were on the right-hand grass verge and saw it smash into the bank before it went up into the air and somersaulted three times. We were already running towards the crash as we saw the driver fall headfirst out of the cockpit onto the wet ground.

By the time we got to him he was unconscious. I checked him over thoroughly, as I had been trained to do.

I was satisfied that everything seemed sound and I couldn't find any broken bones. When the ambulance arrived, bringing a doctor, I was amazed to see him go over to make sure the car was all right. Later I heard he was a member of the Bristol Motor Club and his main interest was in cars.

Our ambulance lieutenant, John Drinkwater, checked the patient again before we put him on the stretcher. He said it was all right to move him. So he was taken to the ambulance tent where he stayed for two hours. When he came round, we asked him how he felt. 'Fine,' he said. He rubbed his head as he got up and went off into the crowd without another word.

He didn't take part in the afternoon racing, but went instead to the first aid tent complaining of pain in the face. Bill Brine was there and he had a quick look at the driver's jaw. 'Do you wear dentures?' he asked.

'Yes, I do.'

'Don't move them whatever you do! Do you use denture cream, or anything like that?'

'Yes, I use a dental fixative.'

'You're a lucky man,' said Bill. 'You've got a broken jaw!'

So they rushed him off to hospital. He had actually broken his jaw in three places and his dentures had held everything together. The hospital staff left the dentures in to act as a splint.

At the next meeting, the driver came into the ambulance tent and we asked him how he was.

'My jaw has healed up well, thanks to your help. They told me at the hospital that if I hadn't had the dentures in place I would probably have had broken blood vessels and all sorts of other complications – and I would have had a lot more pain!'

On one occasion I was on duty at the Bristol Hippodrome. That night the Billy Cotton Band Show was on. In the Hippodrome there were stalls, a grand tier and balcony and in those days people were allowed to smoke in all three parts of the theatre. When you were up near the roof it was quite hot.

During the second house, a man came up to me and asked me if I could see to his wife. It was easy to pick her out in the middle of the row. She was quite flushed and in obvious distress. The seats were made of padded boards and we did our best not to bump her against them as we managed to get her out to the top of a stairway where it was cooler. I found a chair and we sat her down. She was struggling for breath and seemed on the point of fainting.

'How long are you going to be?' the husband asked

'I don't know,' I said. 'Your wife's not fit enough to go back in at the moment.'

'Well, I want to see Billy Cotton. That's what I came for.'

His wife managed to gasp: 'You can go back in if you like, dear.'

He needed no second bidding, but before he turned to go I asked her if she was wearing any tight clothing.

'Yes, I am.'

'Well go into that little closet over there with your husband and take it off.'

When she came out, her waist seemed to have increased by nearly ten inches. As soon as we had sat her down again, her husband went back into the auditorium. She was breathing more deeply now and obviously glad of the relief. I stayed with her and she began telling me that she had been seriously ill in bed for ten weeks with dropsy which had swollen out her stomach. She had got up that afternoon because her husband had bought tickets for the show.

'But you're still very ill,' I said. 'You should never have come tonight.'

'I know, but I didn't want to disappoint him, he can be so difficult.'

Again, she began to gasp for breath and I knew she would need careful handling if she wasn't to be put in danger. When the husband reappeared I led him away from his wife so that we were out of earshot. 'You're not doing your wife any good by bringing her out for the first time like this. Make sure you take her home in a car or a taxi.'

He looked put out by my words. 'I'm afraid she'll have to go home on the bus.'

'She will not,' I said. 'You do as I tell you.' I continued in this vein, making the most of the authority my uniform gave me until he agreed to order a taxi.

When he went off I wondered what I could do to alleviate his wife's distress. I decided to keep her talking so that her mind would be taken off her condition and she was soon telling me about life with her selfish husband. As she unburdened herself her breathing improved and she became calmer.

Just then a girl attendant came out and asked me if I would go and see another patient in the audience.

Back inside she said: 'It's like a mothers' meeting out there. Don't you two chat!'

'I haven't done any chatting. I've only been listening.'

I was convinced that the unfortunate woman would have been in serious difficulties if she hadn't found a sympathetic ear. Healing must include listening. And it surprises me that it should take forty years for this to be recognized as an essential element in patient care.

When the celebrated hypnotist Peter Casson was billed at the Hippodrome, he called a meeting of all the ambulance personnel. He said he needed a full crew every night and our main duties would be to pick up the bodies in the audience. He would be hypnotizing the people who had volunteered to go up on the stage and others in the audience would be dropping like flies. We would have to go and get them out from their seats, take them to the back of the building and lay them out in the hall foyer. He would come round afterwards and revive them. We laughed out loud when he told us this, we thought he was kidding. But we soon found out he wasn't. We would get as many as ten or twelve people from the balcony or gallery and we would have to stretch them out in the foyer.

One night he said: 'If any of you want to come up on stage, you can.'

Not one of us volunteered for that. We didn't want to get hypnotized!

His stage performance was the way he earned his living.

We found out afterwards that he did a lot of healing as well, using the same techniques. This taught me how the power of suggestion can help people who are ill. A hypnotist can do many things, but they cannot work unless you are willing to help them. They can only help people who want to help themselves.

A hypnotist tries to get through to the subconscious mind, the person within. They may not realize it, but that is where they are working. If we, as healers, can get the patient to relax, to allow things to happen and to accept what is happening, we too can get through to their subconscious mind, their spiritual self. Once the link is made, we can help them.

Sometimes our ambulance was called to private houses. I went out with the crew one day to pick up an old man who was going to be put into a nursing home in Salisbury. When we got to the house, his son and daughter were there. They both looked as if they were glad to see the back of the old fellow. We asked the son if he would like to accompany his father in the ambulance.

'I'm not going all the way to Salisbury in the back of an ambulance with him. I'll have to travel in the front.'

The driver shrugged and said: 'If you want, you can go in the back, Dennis, but if you don't want to you can stay in the front.'

I said I would go in the back with the old man and his daughter. I sat next to him and held his hand. He had a pathetic feeling about him. His daughter spent most of the two and a half hour journey running him down, but he seemed pretty harmless to me. By the time we reached the nursing home it was dark outside. We had to carry the stretcher across the grounds of the nursing home which looked bleak and miserable. What a place to end your days in, I thought.

An attendant walked in front with a torch and I was walking behind. The old man hadn't said a word during the journey, but now he raised his head up and said: 'I'm not bad.' He was referring to the horrible man his daughter had been describing.

Suddenly I felt his loneliness as if it were my own. We were going to leave him in this barren place. He put his hand out and gripped mine with the strength of a younger man. 'Thank you for everything,' he said. 'I'll be all right now.'

Did he feel my compassion for him? I would like to think that knowing somebody did care had helped the old man to accept the situation and perhaps even to be able to face the trauma of being institutionalized. Only a small effort is needed to give someone this kind of support.

I was twenty-two then and it would be another twenty years before I started healing. But work as a healer begins long before, perhaps even in childhood. I found that wherever I went, if people were in trouble they would come and talk to me. I used to feel sorry for them and commiserate with them and listen to them and more often than not they would go on their way feeling much happier. In those days I used to get quite miserable and depressed over other people's problems. I didn't know that sympathy creates a link between people, enabling love energy to flow between one person and another. If we don't dismiss their problems from our minds once a healing situation is over, this link allows our energy to drain away so that we begin to feel depleted and we start to take on the problem ourselves. Soon we are feeling as unhappy as they are without being able to understand why.

We have to conserve our energies when we are not healing. Healing energy flows into us and through us and while we are working it seems to build us up. But it is essential to turn off the flow once that energy is no longer needed. I liken this to a car, standing doing nothing until there is a journey to make. Then we turn the key in the ignition and the battery has energy to start. Once the energy has come through and done its work we have finished the job and we need to switch our engine off. In this way we conserve the supply in the battery.

But this was a lesson I had yet to learn.

THREE

Learning to Use the Gift

In the spring of 1949 I was twenty-four and in love with my teenage sweetheart, Dorothy. My job in the metal foundry gave me a regular salary and there was plenty of overtime if I wanted it. We decided to get married and although we had no home of our own to go to we were very happy. By the time we had moved into a new council house four years later, our second child was born. I worked all the overtime I could get to earn enough to look after my new family. I would go to work on the early morning shift and return home late at night.

But this was to prove a mistake. Without realizing what was happening, I was spending more and more time at work and less and less with my wife. It became impossible to plan a social life and there was little time left for entertainment. Normal married life became a luxury I couldn't afford.

As time went by, our relationship inevitably suffered so that after fifteen years I had become a stranger to the woman I loved. In the struggle to make ends meet I had forgotten the struggle to keep my marriage alive, and we finally agreed to part.

This was a tragedy for me at the time and I found myself in the depths of despair. At that point no one could have convinced me that I was in the trough of a wave and that one day I would rise to its crest.

I did not realize it then, but there were signs all around me of the dawning of a new age. In the United States a new movement had begun in the first light of this dawn –

they called it 'Flower Power'. Young people were trying to apply the power of love to the problems of the world in which they found themselves. I doubted whether these long-haired youngsters, dressed in brightly coloured clothes, could solve these problems with love and flowers. But something in my heart stirred. My own life had collapsed around me; I wanted an answer and I wanted the answer to be love.

Now I can see that just as the world was going through the changes which were heralding the age of Aquarius, so indeed was I. The day Billy Thomas said to me 'So you're a healer, Dennis' my life changed again. The trough of the wave was about to surge upwards.

Through going to Spiritualist churches I met Doris, who was to become my second wife. She used to talk to me about healing and spiritual matters and we became good friends. As I told her about various things that had happened in my life, she became convinced that there was a pattern of caring which ran all the way through it.

At the non-ferrous metal company, for example, most of the work involved refining out lead and tin from metal rubbish. During the handling process, soft metal splinters broke off and if they got under the skin they were difficult to get out. They had to be dug out whole or there was a danger of them breaking up and the wound festering. I had worked out a way of removing the splinters with a penknife on which I had fashioned a sharp chisel-shaped edge. I would cut round the splinter, dig underneath and flick it out. Soon all the men were coming to me to have their splinters removed. They never flinched and I never hurt them, whereas other people who had tried apparently did.

I hadn't given this much thought, I was just happy to be able to help them. But Doris saw such things as demonstrating the healing gift. She had heard mediums repeatedly refer to my abilities and when I told her about the woman in the car whose back trouble had been cured, she was not at all surprised. 'Why can't you see it, Dennis? You are a healer. These things shouldn't surprise you. You don't need to know how it happens at this stage. Just

37

get on and do it and build up your experience.'

I knew she was right and I knew that the more I practised the gift, the closer I would get to discovering how it
worked. She understood that most of my reluctance was
due to lack of confidence and low self-esteem. So she
helped me to believe in myself and in my ability to let
spirit energy flow through me. Finally her constant encouragement won through. I stopped making a fuss and
saying that I would rather not, and got into the habit of
saying yes and just doing it.

The accepted method then was for the patient to come in
and sit in front of you without saying anything and 'have
healing'. The healers I had watched then got up and stood
behind the patient and put their hands on the sides of the
head. After a time they would say 'God bless you' and off
the patient would go. So I did the same. If the patient got
better that was fine, but there was very little corroboration
of this.

I went along with this way of working for a while, but
something was urging me to do more. I started talking to
the patients when they arrived and I would ask them
questions. Often I would be inspired to chat to them
during the healing itself. Most people seemed to have
backaches or headaches or an ache in some other part of
the body and these conditions didn't seem too much of a
problem to deal with.

Soon they were bringing other patients with them, asking if I would see them too. Of course I agreed and treated
these new patients in just the same way. Then a week or
two afterwards I would hear that these new patients had
had an incurable cancer, perhaps with only weeks to live,
but they were all right now. I was astounded and excited. I
was beginning to get some feedback and I encouraged
this.

I noticed that people began to relax as soon as they sat
down and once they had felt the comfort of my touch they
relaxed even more. The healing began with this relaxation
that my hands induced.

I was asked to join a healing clinic in Bristol where there

was a healer who used to go down to the church in the evening and work with several helpers like myself. The church was divided up into separate areas using screens so as to give the patients privacy. The waiting room was below the church and when we were ready we rang a bell. A board downstairs showed the receptionist which healer was free and patients would come up in turn.

Even though patients were encouraged to relax and work with any healer, they tended to stick to the same one. Because of this, each healer at the clinic found they had their own 'clientele' and one had to get used to seeing the same faces. I have never believed in their approach since Spirit is the healer and can work through any number of willing hands. Thus, a patient may be treated by more than one healer, just as they may be treated by more than one doctor or specialist.

When the leader of the clinic invited me to join his group, he made it clear that he did not want me to start work on my own too quickly. 'After all,' he said, 'you have only been in the movement a short while, I understand, so we can't expect too much of you. You need time to develop. There's nothing worse than trying to do too much too soon.'

I wondered how Spirit had been able to work through me so far, but I kept quiet and decided I would do whatever he thought best. I wanted to learn and perhaps he had something new to teach me. He seemed reassured by my attitude and explained how he wanted me to assist him. 'We'll start by you giving me some power, Mr Barrett. This means that you stand back and project psychic energy towards me. This will add to the total amount of energy available to the spirits to enable them to work. I had to do this for several years before I was ever allowed to touch a patient. All part of the apprenticeship, you might say.'

He allowed a slight grin to cross his face, but was soon in control again. I grinned back, to hide my amazement. I wasn't looking forward to several years of standing back and 'projecting energy' while someone else got on with the job which I had previously been assured I could do myself.

The first patient came up and sat on the chair. I stood a few feet away while he went behind and put his hands on the patient's neck. He worked 'under control' which means that his spirit helpers came through and took over completely while the healing was going on. Within a few seconds of going under control, his helper began speaking through him, using his voice. 'Come on, work! You're not here to stand doing nothing, work!'

I didn't understand what was happening, but suddenly he was asking me to work. So I said: 'What do you want me to do, then?'

'Put your hands on the patient.'

I was already aware that the patient had a pain in the abdomen so I went over and knelt down and put my hands over the location of the pain. I stayed like that while I felt the energy flowing into him. I could not move my hands while I was touching him; it was just as if they were glued there. Finally the flow of energy ceased and my friend came out of control and back to normal. I was waiting for further instructions from his spirit helper, instead of which he opened his eyes and saw me touching his patient. He stood back from the patient, looking quite startled and annoyed. 'What are you doing there, Mr Barrett?'

'Your helpers told me to come up and put my hands on him where he had a pain,' I said.

'But I told you to stand back and give power.'

'I know you did. But when you're in the army, you obey the last order first and that's what I did. I did what you told me to.'

'Well . . . if they told you, it must be all right.'

I said no more. I could see that the patient was wondering what was going on and it would not help the healing if I caused any embarrassment.

He had a further ten patients that evening and each time I stood back in the usual way. But each time he went under control, his helper said: 'Put your hands on the patient.'

So I did. I put them where I wanted to. They didn't say 'Touch the chest' or 'Touch the shoulders'; it was left up to me to sense where my hands needed to be put. I was conscious, as soon as I did this, of the flow of energy through my hands into the patient.

At the end of the evening my friend seemed nonplussed, but of course he wouldn't go against what his spirit helpers had asked for. As we put our coats on to go home, he drew me on one side.

'I shall be on holiday next week, Mr Barrett, but Jim will be in charge. I'm sure he'll take care of you while I'm away. Thank you for your, er – help.'

Jim was his second-in-command and he had no reservations about my previous experience. When I turned up the following week he made his attitude quite clear. 'You're not watching me work. There's an empty stool, you use it. Any patients that come up who aren't heading for me or the others, you deal with them, Dennis.'

'Even if they're new patients?'

'New or old, treat them all just the same.'

So he believed in throwing me in at the deep end and seeing if I could swim. Although I had very little idea what I would do with each patient when they arrived, it seemed that I hit the nail right on the head immediately. As soon as they sat down I started to work and I put my hands on them wherever I felt inspired to do so. That night I dealt with ten patients.

The last one had to be helped up the stairs. Her friends were almost carrying her. They sat her down and I was impressed to stand behind her and put my hands on her head. Then I gently let them slide down to her shoulders where I allowed them to rest for almost ten minutes. I said 'God bless you' and she stood up. I could see that she had been crying and was still in an emotional state.

'Are you all right?' I asked.

She blinked back her tears and managed to say: 'Oh, yes, I'm quite all right, thank you.'

I watched her as she walked to the stairs unaided. I had forgotten that she had been carried in a little while before.

The following week, the leader of the healing clinic was there to greet me.

'I hear you were doing healing last week, Mr Barrett.'

'Yes. I did what Jim asked me to.'

'Well, it's all right. But I don't believe in mixing patients and healers. If anybody comes this week who was here last week and you saw them, you carry on seeing them. They're your patients now. And, er – if you *do* have any spare time, you can come and work with me again.'

I had a few new patients and some of those I had seen the previous week turned up again. One of these was the woman who had gone home in tears. When she had sat down she said: 'I'm glad to see you again, Mr Barrett. You don't know what was wrong with me last week, do you?'

'No, I don't. But it doesn't really matter does it, because hopefully you're all right now.'

'Well, yes, I am all right now.'

'That's good.'

'For a long time, almost ten years, I haven't been able to be touched by anything or anybody unless I've had my tablets. I had hypersensitive nerves in the skin. I had to take the tablets even during the night or I wouldn't have been able to stand the feel of the bedclothes against my body. And as for human contact, that was impossible. My husband hasn't been able to put his arms round me all that time. I was only able to wear clothes because I had the tablets inside me.'

She then went on to say that the night I had seen her she had been waiting so long downstairs, she had gone more than the prescribed four hours so there was no tablet active in her system at the time. 'You put your hands straight on me and it didn't hurt or irritate me. I went home and I put my hands round my husband and we just held each other. We held each other, Mr Barrett, and we cried and cried.'

She came several more times. On the third time she said 'I have a confession to make. I hope you won't be angry, but I'm a fraud.'

'A fraud? How do you make that out, then?'

'Well, I don't really need to come here any more, but I keep on coming because I like it so much!'

Nearly everyone in the room looked round when they heard our laughter.

A week after this, a patient had just gone downstairs and I had pressed the bell, when the leader's wife came up. She was a local medium and she had been to a service about a mile away to give clairvoyance. During the course of her work she had been drawn to a woman in the congregation and felt she needed healing. After the service she told the woman that she was going back to a healing clinic that evening and asked if she would like to come.

'I feel this is a case for you, Dennis. She's waiting downstairs. Can I go and fetch her?'

'Of course. What's the problem?'

'That's between you and her.'

She came back with the woman and left after introducing us. I asked her to sit down and found myself being directed to kneel at her side instead of standing behind her. I put my arm across her shoulders and said: 'Come on, then, what's the matter? There's nothing wrong with you.' (Spirit had told me there was nothing physically wrong with her.)

She started to choke a little before she could speak clearly. She wasn't worried about herself, she said, she was worried about her daughter. They had been to a holiday camp together and her daughter had been attacked and raped by three men. She had since gone nearly seven weeks without a period so she was convinced she was pregnant.

My helpers came through strongly. I said: 'I'm very sorry to hear about your daughter and I don't know what to do. But anything that baffles me, I say a prayer about it and hope I shall get the answers afterwards. So how do you feel about praying?'

'I'm a medium myself, but I can't pray any more. I've even lost the words of the Lord's Prayer. I'm so choked up and confused I can't remember the words any more. I'm so frightened about what this has done to us both.'

'All right, then,' I said, 'we'll start praying together. That's about all I can think of.'

I didn't know of a treatment for suspected pregnancy in the case of a multiple rape, but what I did know was that the power of prayer would give absent healing to the situation.

At the back of the church was a fireplace with a gas fire in it to heat the hall. On the mantelpiece above was an illuminated cross in a circular frame. I suggested that we went and sat at the back of the church underneath this cross.

'Would you like to begin or shall I?' I asked her.

She was still too choked up. 'I'm sorry, I couldn't.'

So I said a very simple, very stumbling prayer which included the words 'This is something we can't cope with, will you please take it over?'. It was all I could think of saying. We stayed together there for a few minutes linking hands and then she pressed my hand.

'Thank you,' she said, and was gone.

I went on with the next case. This is one of the principles of healing. It was no longer my problem. You wash your hands of the problem and go on to the next one. If you don't do this you can get very confused.

Three weeks later the woman came back to tell me that she had gone home that night feeling as if all her burdens had been lifted from her shoulders. She had gone to bed and slept soundly for the first time in weeks. In the morning her daughter woke her up with a cup of tea and a smile on her face.

'I'm all right, Mum,' she said.

Her period had arrived.

This was the way things were in the beginning. Spirit was giving me so much evidence, I couldn't doubt it. Even so I had butterflies in my stomach with every new case. I wasn't worried about my spirit helpers letting me down, I was more worried that I would let them down.

Round about this time, Doris and I were introduced to the widow of a blind medium called Ricky. She had been a tremendous support to him and was truly the power behind the throne. Since he had died a year before, she had done her best to fulfil his bookings and the rest of his commitments. She didn't enjoy being in the public eye and by the time we all met it was becoming more and more of a struggle.

Eunice invited us over and it was at her house that I began the next stage of my development. The three of us and her sister-in-law would sit together for hours talking about Spiritualism and spiritual matters. Letters had continued to arrive addressed to her late husband. Those which she didn't know how to answer she handed to me. I would hold them and practice psychometry. This involves clearing the mind and allowing the vibrations of the object to penetrate so that they may be understood. After this I would be able to answer the letters without reading them. When I wrote the replies, I wouldn't allow her to touch them or read them. It soon became obvious, when the correspondents wrote back, that my replies had been exactly what was required.

These activities led quite naturally to the four of us coming together from time to time to make a circle. We used to call it 'having a party'. This meant that we would sit round together in comfortable chairs in a comfortable position. One of us would begin to pray, asking for those in the circle to be protected and for those who loved us to draw closer. This created a spiritual atmosphere and a feeling of unity among the group. Then every member of the circle relaxed completely to allow the mind to clear. The psychic senses were then able to pick up the higher vibrations of those in Spirit.

Eunice's husband Ricky, and other friends, started to draw closer to us and on occasions would take control of either one of us. Her sister-in-law never really joined in, but she always enjoyed what happened. One of the women might be speaking in her own voice and the next moment another voice would come through. It might be Ricky or almost anyone because we were so free and easy we could let them come through without any trouble. Among other things, Ricky taught me that communication with those in Spirit is perfectly natural. There is nothing sanctimonious or nonsensical about it. It is exactly like communicating with any other human being.

Towards the end of the year Ricky came through and said: 'My spirit friends and I are coming here to celebrate the festive season with my beloved.'

We didn't know then that we also had an invitation for
Christmas. He was speaking through Doris at the time.
During the course of a long conversation I asked Ricky if
we would have a 'party'.

'Yes, I hope so.'

'Are we going to have any singers?' asked. 'I'd like to
have a good singsong.'

'All right,' he said, 'who would you like?'

I named a number of famous singers including Caruso,
Galli-Curci, people like that. 'Any of them will do me, I'm
not greedy!'

We all had a good laugh at this. (We used to joke with
each other all the time.)

Ricky laughed too. 'I'll do my best,' he said and it was
time for him to go.

Before we left that night, Doris and I were invited to
stay for Christmas.

On Christmas Day we had a wonderful time. There was
a good spread with plenty to drink as well. The hours
passed quickly and we entertained each other far into the
evening. It was nearly midnight when I decided to go to
bed. I always take messages from Spirit with a pinch of
salt so I didn't really expect any great singers to come
through any of us that day, and so far they hadn't.

I went to the bathroom on my way to the bedroom and
no one could have been more surprised than I when I
came out singing at the top of my voice. I returned to the
living room, singing as I went, and before very long they
had all joined in with me. Each of us had controls coming
through, but we were aware of what was going on so we
could enjoy the singing. I sang every voice, male and
female, soprano, bass and tenor and I thoroughly enjoyed
it.

Eunice's sister-in-law sat in the corner and listened in
amazement. The performance lasted over three hours
during which we sang opera, ballads and folksongs from
many countries. Finally we fell into bed and I slept long
and deeply.

We were woken up on Boxing Day morning by a knock
on the door. The house was a prefab, detached from all

the others, and somebody was asking how we had got such a big choir into such a small house! The enquiries continued. Apparently half the street had stayed up all night listening to the amazing choir. It had been a Christmas to remember. Ricky had certainly done his best!

Doris wanted to be more involved in my healing nights so we began to work together. She would hold the patient's hands so that energy could flow round the body, helping them to relax and feel more confident. Meanwhile I could go to work on the patient's problem.

It soon became obvious, however, that there were more than enough healers at the clinic and the leader was hoping one of us would drop out. We heard about another clinic which needed new healers so we decided to work with them.

This was held in the upper room of a Co-op hall on Wednesday evenings and forty to fifty patients were turning up each week. The waiting area and healing area were all on the same level. There were no screens and people would simply come out and sit on one of the stools at the front of the hall. The leader of the healing group was a man called Maurice Flook. His custom was to take us all into the kitchen before the session started for a prayer. Then we went in and took patients as they came. They were encouraged to come to whichever healer was free, but Maurice did sometimes direct patients to a specific healer if they were not going to him.

On my first night there he pointed to me and helped the patient over. The man was using crutches. He moved by bringing his left foot up to the right one and then flinging the right leg forward.

'Dennis, this is John. I saw him last week. I'd like you to deal with him.'

John sat down in front of me and Doris held his hands. His story was that during the war he had been badly injured in the Blitz. Masonry had fallen on him, smashing his pelvis and breaking his right leg into many pieces which had subsequently fused together. I was allowed to see the x-rays some time afterwards. It looked as if the pel-

47

vis and bones in the right leg were covered in feint hairlines from hip to toe, giving the appearance of hundreds
of interlocking pieces of a jigsaw puzzle.

'Well, we'll see what we can do, John.'

Immediately I felt my spirit helper coming through. But
this was a new one. Up until then I hadn't known who my
helpers were, but this one felt like a very large man. I work
in my shirtsleeves without a tie, which was just as well
because he turned out to be a Zulu, seven feet four inches
tall. People in the hall saw me expand and grow. All the
buttons on my shirt popped off, just like when David Banner turns into the Incredible Hulk. But my hips became
narrow and my trousers began to slide down. Doris told
me afterwards they were afraid my trousers were going to
disappear altogether, such was the effect of my growing
into the shape of this new helper who was a foot taller
than myself, but all shoulders and no hips!

I bent down to John's level and my spirit helper set to
work on him in a way which I had experienced neither
before nor since. My hand went right the way round his
thigh, even though he was a big man of about 220 pounds,
and then across his hip. It was as if I surrounded the bones
with my hand. As I wrenched, pulled, twisted and
snapped them, I felt myself becoming hotter and hotter.
My hands moved down to his knee and did the same,
working it, stretching it and snapping it. Then the foot
was given a similar treatment.

After half an hour I felt the movement beneath my
hands slow down and opened my eyes. Everything was
drenched in perspiration and I felt wonderful. Apparently
people had been waiting for John to cry out in agony, but
he had spent the whole time grinning like a Cheshire cat.

'How's that, then?' I asked him.

'Lovely!' he said and stood up without any assistance.
He allowed his weight to shift on to the left leg and raised
the right leg up and moved his foot. He turned to me,
beaming. 'I haven't been able to do this since that day
during the war. It's incredible!'

The thing that impressed me was that he had control as
well as mobility. Although he had to walk with care, now

he could walk using both feet. I saw him to the top of the stairs and he managed to get down them quite reasonably. It was only then that I noticed the state of my clothes. I had resumed my normal shape and size, but they were in quite a mess. I chuckled as Doris described what had been happening.

John came back the following week for more treatment and I saw him for six weeks, during the course of which he asked my helpers questions. One of the questions was: 'Should I have a built-up boot because my right leg is one and a quarter inches shorter than the other?' He was aware of the fact that at the age of fifty-six bones don't normally continue growing. The answer he got from my helpers was: 'Why don't you wait until your leg grows, then see what your doctor says?'

'Will I be able to walk properly again?'

'Let's hope so.'

'Will I be able to run for a bus too?'

'If your walking improves, why not?'

I asked John why he had wanted to be able to run for a bus. He said it had always annoyed him that he couldn't run for a bus if he was a little behind and he had to stand and watch it go without him.

'I really would love to be able to run for a bus one day.'

Was there anything else he would like to ask, I wondered. 'I used to be very fond of swimming. Would I be able to swim again?'

'Try it!' came the firm answer.

Some months after this, he brought along the x-rays which showed the bones before and after. The hairlines had become less prominent and there was actually a ball and socket joint in the hip where there had formerly been only a mass of interlocking pieces.

'This is wonderful,' I said. 'What's been happening to you then, John?'

He told us how his walking had improved day by day and eventually he went back to see the specialist. The specialist said he was going to have him measured for a boot, whether he liked it or not.

John said: 'What do I need a boot for?'

The specialist looked at his notes. 'To make up for the difference in the length of your legs. It'll help you to walk better. Why are you asking, anyway, we've gone into this before?'

'Well, there's nothing wrong with my legs.'

The specialist hadn't noticed that John now had a mobile leg so he said: 'We'll see about that. Get up on the couch. The nurse will help you.'

'It's all right. I can manage.' And John jumped onto the couch. The specialist was more than surprised and got his measuring instruments out. He found a quarter of an inch discrepancy between the two legs where it had been one and a quarter inches before; his leg had grown one inch in the few months since I had seen him. The specialist was speechless when John brought his leg up and wiggled his foot in his face.

We couldn't help laughing at John's happiness and the sparkle in his eye.

'That's not all. I've been swimming and I can do the full breaststroke. It's as if life has just started again. Everything you said has come true.'

'Even running for the bus?'

'I had a go quite soon after I last saw you. The bus was already at the stop and I decided to run for it. I waved to the conductor, but he just rang the bell and it pulled away. But I was running!'

Maurice hadn't directed John to me by chance. Though shorter than I, he too had a Zulu helper whose name was Mgombe. Mgombe was apparently from the same tribe as my helper.

'They're blood brothers, Dennis. Your helper is called Mfollo. I enjoyed watching him come through you. It reminded me of the day I was working as a medium at Knowle church. I was on the rostrum standing under this fluorescent light when Mgombe came through. I grew so tall, I knocked the light with my head. This was in front of the congregation!'

It was a relief to know that someone else had experienced the same physical phenonemon. If I hadn't heard the testimony of so many witnesses and seen the evidence of my own clothes, I wouldn't have believed that such a change could be brought about in the body.

At that time I was working seven miles down the river at Avonmouth. The Portway was hardly busy then and I had a nice clear run on my motorbike. One day I was riding home thinking about the whole reality of Spirit coming through a person and what they could do. What would happen if they came through on a motorbike, I wondered. Would they be able to ride it? What would happen if a man as big as Mfollo came through while I was on this motorbike, for instance?

As if in answer to my thoughts, the bike seemed to shrink. It felt like a toy beneath me as I swelled. I was driving with the handlebars between my knees and I was looking down at the road from a distinctly elevated position. I continued to drive for several miles like that, feeling quite cheerful and happy. I drove along in the normal way, adjusting the throttle without thinking about it. No one else was around.

Then I had a moment of panic. When would I return to my normal size? Sooner or later I would pass somebody and what would they think? A car was coming towards me. The driver looked across as we passed, and I heard the squeal of tyres as he accelerated away. Eventually I returned to my normal physical dimensions before I arrived home.

That night we were having a 'party' with some friends. I told them about the fun on the way home and they doubled up with laughter at the thought of the poor driver seeing this huge man completely dwarfing his motorbike. Laughter always raises the vibrations, just as being miserable or depressed lowers them, and this helped to create ideal conditions for our spirit friends to come through. As always we let ourselves go and who should come but my own spirit helper, talking through one of the circle.

This helper made it quite clear that he was aware of what had happened to me on the motorbike and that he would like to take the opportunity to give us a little teaching, saying that they too had found the incident amusing.

'It is important for you to realize,' he said, 'that we can use every faculty you possess, every capability, every item of knowledge. All we need is the chance, the invitation. This is what you need to understand because this is what it means to be a channel for Spirit. You have given us the freedom to use you, but never forget that you always have the power of veto. You can block anything that does not feel right to you. For example, we wouldn't expect to be allowed to speak through Dennis Barrett in a foreign tongue because it would sound like gibberish to him. But you do have the capacity to drive a motorbike or a car. It is sometimes necessary for us to use this facility.'

The experiences we had in such home circles taught me that there is no need to stand on ceremony with our spirit helpers. If, for instance, they came through and we didn't understand what they were trying to say, we would tell them so. If they said something we thought was far-fetched we would say: 'We'll take that with a pinch of salt.' They are human like us and fallible like us. It is important to be aware of each entity's level of understanding before accepting every word they say. They are people, not ghosts. If I ever saw a ghost, I would be the first to run the three-minute mile!

Holding the patient's hands was as far as Doris ever got while she was working with me. It was her own attitude which decided this. She had taken a dislike to a certain woman some years before. This person was younger than either of us and very attractive. I knew her and I had always managed to get on with her. One evening she came to the clinic for healing. As Doris saw her approaching she became very agitated. 'I've got to go down to the car. I can't stay here.'

I asked her to wait until the session was finished, but she became more and more distressed and finally stormed out of the hall. I was upset by her behaviour, but I had to control my feelings as quickly as possible in order to work. The problem would have to be sorted out later when I got home.

The woman came and sat down and told me that she

had had an accident while out riding. She had fallen off a horse and impacted her fingers, two of which had become completely stiff. Movement in the other fingers was severely restricted. Fortunately for her this was her only injury.

Mfollo the Zulu came through and worked on her hand. He seemed to probe the joints gently, directing energy into them until they became free. After twenty minutes, all her fingers were moving and she left with a grateful smile.

I had been completely thrown by Doris's dramatic exit and it marked the end of our partnership in public healing. A week later, I attended the clinic on my own.

I had sold the motorbike and we only had one car between us. By some coincidence the car was never available to me on Wednesday evenings. This meant that I would have to make the difficult journey by public transport. Finally, to avoid any further arguments at home, I decided to give up my work at the clinic. Maurice thought I was making a mistake, but he could understand the position I was in.

'You're a healer, Dennis,' he said. 'You won't stop working now they've got you started. They'll find a way.'

And they did. I had managed to build up a reputation in Bristol. If people couldn't see me at the clinic, they found their way to my home. And these visits helped to lay the foundations of my own healing practice which continues to this day.

FOUR

Think Pink!

When I look back over the years since my healing practice began, many hundreds of cases come to mind, covering many of the health problems which beset humanity. From the simplest headache to the most devastating physical or mental illnesses, the one golden light that has made itself so obvious to me is the power or energy of love, the God force, that animates all things. Without this, nothing can exist. It is the source of the energy that Spirit utilizes in the healing process and it is at all times an expression of love. From the positive application of this love energy, all forms of love are derived. These include, of course, sympathy, empathy, compassion, the urge to care and nurture, the desire to heal as well as healing itself.

I find it a wonderful thing that each and every one of my patients has played a part in teaching me about the power of love and its spiritual source. It would be difficult, there-fore, to say that a particular person has brought me more than any other. The cases I mention in this book have been picked out to illustrate certain points. They are not isolated incidents, but part of the tapestry of my life into which all my patients are woven. Many of them I will never meet. They may have written or telephoned from distant parts of the world and cannot travel to see me, but the link has been made.

Since I have never advertised, it would be true to say that my healing practice depends on word of mouth so this link probably exists between all of them. Some of the links have brought me travel at home and abroad, leading to new experiences and new friends. When a patient calls here or writes to me for healing, I have never known where that first contact would lead. This is part of the fun in my life. The other element of excitement is actually working with my spirit helpers for they have ensured that every day is a new adventure in living.

In the late seventies I was spending a good deal of time answering correspondence from people who had heard about me. One of these letters was from the publisher, Oliver Caldecott. In it he told me about his wife, Moyra, who had been seriously ill in hospital. Although she was quite young, she was severely restricted and confined in everything she did because of chronic angina. It was a great shame because she had so much potential to enjoy life, but she was completely handicapped by her condition. Was there anything I could do?

At that time I used to send out pre-printed letters to people whom I didn't know which explained the general principles of healing. On the back I would write something more personal. On this occasion, in my reply to Oliver Caldecott, I enclosed an envelope addressed to Moyra. My helpers dictated a letter which said that I wanted her to keep the envelope separately and not to let anyone else handle it, since it was her personal link with spirit healing. Any time she had a problem with her condition she was to get the letter out and either hold it or read it. I made an appointment for her to come to see me and said that I would be giving her absent healing in the meantime. If all went well I would look forward to seeing her in about two weeks.

The appointed day came and she and Oliver arrived by car. When she walked in I could see she had already made an improvement. I asked her to lie down on the healing couch and my helpers came through and took over. I held my hands just above her chest. As the spirits went to work they told her they would be using an ultrasonic form of energy to disperse the deposits around her arteries.

The treatment lasted for about half an hour. Afterwards Moyra described it as a fluttering feeling in her chest. She had come with many questions in her mind which she did not put to me, but had been amazed to find them answered one by one as my helpers talked to her during the treatment. I advised her to rest for three days when she would start to notice a change in her condition, but I would need to see her for a second treatment.*

Moyra didn't feel better until the fourth day when she found she could lift a kettle. This was something she could only do with difficulty. When she came for her second appointment I told her she had been too ill to be healed in one treatment. Spirit used ultrasonic energy on her again and this time the last traces of the condition were cleared.

Of course she was eventually summoned to see the specialist for a check-up. She told him she had been receiving treatment from a spirit healer and was feeling a lot better. He suggested that she should undergo the usual tests, just to be on the safe side. Moyra said she neither needed them nor did she want them. So he suggested the ultimate test which was to put her on an exercise bike. He told her that at the first sign of distress she should ring the bell and he would come at once. Whereupon he left the room.

Half an hour later she was still pedalling when he came in and said: 'Get off, Mrs Caldecott. You're fitter than I am!'

The hospital entered Moyra's recovery as 'spontaneous remission', without recording that she had been to a healer. Interestingly, the use of ultrasonics as a therapeutic tool by the medical profession would not come until many years later.

Moyra's return to health was so spectacular that she was invited to talk about it on local radio programmes and she has since been mentioned in a number of books. As a result of this publicity, people have asked her for my address. Funnily enough, by the time many of them get

---

* Among the novels she has written since, Moyra describes a healing based on her experiences at the time in *The Temple of the Sun* (Rex Collings, 1977) and more recently in *The Green Lady and the King of Shadows* (Gothic Image Publications, 1989).

here they have already begun to improve so I think they have received some healing from her. She has such a lovely, caring personality.

Some time later, I received an illegible letter from a professor who was a specialist in the hospital where Moyra had been treated. I had no idea what he wanted, but I was able to gather his address from the letter heading. I wrote to him giving an appointment and suggesting that he should ring if this was not convenient.

He arrived on time accompanied by his wife and I asked him to lie down on the healing couch. He said he was due to have an operation on his prostate gland and that he also needed treatment for a problem in the rectal area. He didn't want to go through with the operation because he knew what happened in the operating theatre in such cases. In his opinion, patients got better *in spite of* the surgeon's work with the knife and not because of it. He described the pains in his groin and back passage and asked if I could help him.

As always, I said that I couldn't promise anything, but I would do my best. Immediately my helpers came through and set to work, describing what they were doing. They had to 'tidy up' the area at the base of the bladder, which they did. Then they described the cleaning out of the lower intestines, particularly the rectum. The professor listened carefully to all this and nodded from time to time, but he didn't say if he was aware of anything going on. After I had finished we sat and chatted together for another half hour and they left for London.

I heard no more from him for several weeks when I received a short letter which this time I could just about decipher. It read: 'Thank you for trying to help me. I know it is not possible to help everybody. Yours, etc.'

I was disappointed by the inconclusive tone and would have liked to know whether he felt better. Feedback is essential to the healer. I always like to know if my work is successful or not, but so often I only hear from a patient if my help is needed again. However, it is not part of a healer's job to worry about a patient, so I dismissed the letter

57

from my mind.

Three years later I arranged an appointment for a Swiss woman who was visiting England. I asked her how she had heard about me and she said she was a friend of the professor's wife. She had told her to come and see me because I had done so much good for her husband! I held my breath.

'What else did she say?' I asked. 'He had been due to go into hospital for an operation the week after he saw me.'

'So they didn't tell you what happened? He never went for that operation. He didn't need to. He's as fit as a fiddle. His wife says he's as good a lover as he ever was when he was a young man!'

I have since found out that this professor has recommended me to many patients who have come here from all over the country. He has asked them not to mention his name, though sometimes they let it out. But this is the best endorsement of my work that he could give me.

Clairvoyant people have told me they can see my spirit helpers working with me. One of these is a tall Chinese man, known as the Honourable Chang. He is over six foot, thin and angular, with a drooping moustache, dressed in the robes of a high official of the Imperial Court. The first time he ever came through, I didn't know who he was until he introduced himself during a healing session and allowed the patient to talk to him.

I had arranged to meet this woman at her friend's house on the south side of Bristol. She had had every treatment available for very bad asthma and was now on the strongest dosage of drugs that could be allowed without killing her. She was allergic to pet fish in a tank, ordinary house dust and anything made of wool. She was also being treated for this allergic condition by her doctor. Her husband wasn't very interested in healing so I had arranged to see the woman with her friend as chaperone.

Her friend had done what she could to relax the patient, but I was aware that, in spite of the drugs, she was still in a state of high anxiety. I asked her to sit on a dining chair and put my hands on her head. Chang came through straight away and she remarked that she could feel a current of energy coming from my hands.

'It's stimulating, yet very soothing at the same time,' she said.

I knew that Chang was working almost entirely on her nervous system, especially in the region of the solar plexus. I still didn't know who my helper was and when he began speaking to her I was startled by this new voice. In a few moments he had triggered off a great emotional release in her and she began to cry with deep, heaving sobs. I put my arms around her and my shirt was soon saturated with scalding hot tears. I looked over at her friend. She seemed a little apprehensive, but Chang was cheering her on.

'Go on, go on!' he urged. 'Ladies like to cry, you cry!'

So she wept until she could weep no more. Eventually Chang stopped working on her and asked her how she felt.

'That was wonderful,' she said. 'I enjoyed that!'

Chang said he was pleased she had let herself go and we arranged to meet again the following week at her own house on the outskirts of Bristol. Her husband was going to be on the afternoon shift at work from two until ten, so we could go up in the evening without offending him.

When I turned up at the house I walked into the living room to find the husband sitting there. He had changed his shifts because he wanted to see what we were doing and how we had done it. After the introductions were over, the door opened and the three children came in and sat down, watching us like the three wise monkeys. No one seemed to know what to say so I turned to the children. 'You know I've come here to help your mummy, don't you? You aren't going to be afraid, are you?'

The eldest child said, 'Oh, no. You help my mummy if you can. We want to stay and watch.'

I said that was fine and I didn't ask any questions about how their mother had been during the past week. I sat her in an upright chair as usual and began to work. Chang came through and as soon as I touched her she started weeping loudly as if her heart was broken. Again, it was a great emotional release. Chang cheered her on and I could feel a surge of energy around us as if her husband and children were cheering her on too. Finally his work was finished and he introduced himself to her.

'I am the Honourable Chang, but "Chang" to my friends and you are my friends. I am the instrument's helper. I have been so happy to be able to help you.'

She dried her eyes and now both she and her husband overwhelmed us with their news and their questions. They were excited by all the changes that had come about so rapidly. She had been feeling wonderful all week and she hadn't needed to use her respirator. They were intrigued by Chang's introduction.

'Who is "the instrument" – do you mean Mr Barrett?'

'Yes. He is the healing instrument through whom we can work.'

'But . . . who are *you*? You are a spirit helper working through Mr Barrett, and you're Chinese?'

'I am his helper in Spirit. When I was on the earth plane, when I lived here, I was a Chinese mandarin. Now I practise the healing arts in the world of Spirit, a world which is on a higher vibration than this one. This is why I appear to be invisible and inaudible to your ordinary senses.'

'You speak through Mr Barrett so that we can hear you, then?'

'This is so. I would like you to understand that because I come from the world of Spirit, which is your true home, I have far greater resources to draw on in order to heal. These resources are therefore available to you. But, like you, I am still human.'

The children seemed satisfied by all they had seen and heard and got up and went out to play. Her husband thanked me and they both asked me if I or 'we' would keep on coming. I said we would.

Within six weeks they were planning a trip to Cornwall at the height of the pollen season. Before they went she wanted to be given a clean bill of health by her doctor. She told him what had been happening and he assured her that he knew all about spirit healing.

'I'm going to give you the check-up of your life. We'll

see about this spirit healing.'

So she underwent every test he could think of, until finally he held out his hand. 'Give me back all the tablets I've prescribed for you. You don't need them, you're in perfect health.'

At this point she panicked. 'But how will I manage if I need them and I haven't got them, doctor?'

'If you need them and you're anywhere in England, telephone me and I'll drive through the night and deliver them to you. Failing this, I'll arrange with local physicians to see that you have the right tablets. But as far as I can tell, you no longer need any of them.'

It was a hot summer and she enjoyed her fortnight in Cornwall. The holiday boosted her confidence so much that she took a job in a dry cleaner's and found that she was unaffected by the fumes.

Several months after the healing I received a letter from her which said: 'I have caught a bad cold and I am afraid it will develop into asthma and I will be back to square one. Is there any chance you can come and see me?'

I called round the next morning and she said there was a second letter in the post for me. She had woken up feeling wonderful again and knew the asthma couldn't return. Since she had last seen me she had taken up knitting and the children had bought themselves a fish tank.

'I feel a bit mean getting you over here under false pretences, but I'm glad to see you again,' she said.

Doris and I had got married in 1970. However, after four years, I still had difficulty trying to reconcile myself to my divorce from Dorothy. This helped to undermine our relationship, which was gradually becoming untenable. We wanted to remain friends and not end up disliking each other so we agreed to go our separate ways. I moved over to North Bristol where I live now and where the practice is situated.

The place was quite cold and draughty. One Saturday evening I was thinking of going out, but I put my head outside the door to find it tipping down with rain. This can put people off calling on me so I decided to stay in, carry on unpacking and watch the wrestling on television.

The programme had just started when there was a ring on the doorbell. On the doorstep stood a young woman in her late twenties. She had walked through the rain and her clothes were soaked. I recognized her because her mother was a local medium.

'Mum told me to come and see you. She said you could help me.'

'I'm sorry. I can't give you any treatment without someone else present. Where is your mother right now?'

'At home.'

'She knows very well I don't see women on their own. I can't help you. Go and get your mother or bring somebody else with you and I'll see what I can do.'

She stood there looking at me with the rain running off her and tears welling up in her eyes.

'Oh, all right,' I said. 'Come in and have a cup of tea anyway.'

She came in and sat down and I gave her a towel to dry herself while I made her a cup of tea. She told me how she had just lost a baby and had miscarried two others so she was very depressed and unhappy. Her marriage was suffering considerably as a result and both she and her husband were tense and anxious. She went on to describe their arguments and how sex was becoming a chore. They had tried hard to get her pregnant and each time she had been unable to carry the baby.

As I sat and listened to her story, my thoughts turned to absent healing. I knew that just being a sympathetic listener was a form of healing, but this situation needed more than this. Absent healing worked over any distance, including a few feet, so why not in this case? I noticed that she was beginning to calm down and had stopped clutching at her clothes.

I told her that the first priority was to relax. She was uptight and there was no way she could conceive and carry a child for the full term while she was in this tense state. If she could relax, her husband would feel more relaxed himself. They had both focused their anxieties on the act of love so that it was a stressful situation where making a baby was more important than loving. I suggested that she should try and see the whole of their time together as an act of love and join in wholeheartedly with living a life with her husband. She should make love because she was in love, not because she wanted a baby. Their lovemaking should be the pleasure and joy of giving to each other and if she conceived then the baby would be a bonus.

We spent another hour together talking about herself and the principles of living. Finally she went away reassured and relaxed and I didn't hear from her for nearly a year. Then out of the blue came a telephone call asking me to be godfather to her first baby. Apparently she had gone home that night full of happiness and there had been a better harmony between her and her husband than there ever had been before. She conceived almost immediately and carried the baby for the full term, giving birth to a thriving girl.

'Are you happy?' I asked her.

'Oh, yes!'

'Well a happy mother makes a happy child, so she's a lucky little girl.'

Not long after they had another daughter and the two children are like identical twins, both beautiful with lovely personalities. I have met their mother many times since and she is very active in the community. She is helping people by spreading the word about relaxation and passing her happiness on.

This is how this form of healing works. It has so many implications in daily life. If we can learn to relax in tense or aggressive situations we are, in effect, bringing healing into those situations. We are living in times when our uptight society has been stretched to the limit. Anyone who can relax is helping to relieve the tension and just as tension is contagious, so is relaxation. We have an effect on people.

We have an effect when we project the energy of love. We also have an effect when this energy is used in a negative way, as the power of hate. People who use power in this way tend to forget the law of cause and effect which means that sooner or later the effect will be visited on them.

Sometimes unpleasant things go on in houses because of the use of negative power. This has nothing to do with Spirit for it is human beings on the earth plane who have been manipulating this power for their own evil ends. Mysterious happenings may also be due to other causes such as a spirit who is drawn by some occurrence which took place in the house while they were on the earth plane or because they wish to help those who are now living there.

I was asked to go to a house in Bristol where both of these manifestations were occurring at the same time, although the residents weren't aware of this. As far as they were concerned, there were just some disturbing and rather spooky happenings in the place. The problem was further complicated by the fact that the evil effect of negative power was also present in another house in the family and it was to this house that I was first called.

It was around eight in the evening when I arrived at the house in question where a young woman was living with her five-year-old daughter. Her husband had left them, but her mother lived nearby with her fourteen-year-old stepson. She had asked if they could all be present at the meeting. What the young woman had to tell me sounded like something out of a ghost story. As I listened to her description, I kept an eye on the little girl for she was at an age when children are quite normally aware of anything happening on a psychic level. They heard noises at night which woke them up, including banging doors and hammering on the floor. They started at a set time and went on until four in the morning. Furthermore, this pattern of activity continued every night.

The little girl agreed with this, when her grandmother interrupted to say that similar things were happening in her house. There were also parts of the upper staircase that neither the dogs nor herself nor her stepson could pass. The door to the boxroom couldn't be opened during these times even though it wasn't locked. This was corroborated by her stepson. Both households were obviously distressed by unpleasant and apparently inexplicable events.

If the incidents are linked in some way, my spirit helpers will need to be detectives to solve this one, I thought.

I told the young woman that I would check over her house first if she would lead the way. Before we did so she asked me to wait while she fetched something. She came back with a framed picture. 'I've been wondering about this, Mr Barrett. Could this cause trouble in a house?'

She was holding out a framed pencil drawing of a grotesque and horrifying image. A bestial-looking creature with horns sat enthroned. Its expression was one of cruelty and anger.

'My husband gave me this before he left. He said it was valuable and I might be able to get something for it.'

My intuition was to say: 'Get it out of here, get it out of the house!'

'There's a shed in the garden. Do you mean somewhere like that?'

'Yes, all right. That'll do for the moment. Just get it out of this house.'

She was taken aback by my insistence, but went straight out and put it in the shed. When she came back, I looked over the whole house and couldn't feel any presences of any kind. She suggested that perhaps this was because it wasn't late enough for the happenings to take place so I assured her that I would still be able to feel something if it originated in the house.

'We'd better go to your mother's house now and see what's going on there.'

It only took a few minutes for us to walk round there and this time things were different. As I worked my way to the top of the house, I began to pick up a variety of sensations. I felt something on the stairs, but something stronger was drawing me across the landing to the box-room. I began checking out this room carefully and found an area on a shelf which I didn't like. I asked the grandmother what had been kept on the shelf and she said that her daughter had asked her to store some framed photographs for her while she was moving. She had put them all on the shelf. One of them had been a pencil drawing of some ancient god, she thought.

'The photographs are all right, but the picture was the one I saw in your daughter's house earlier on. It looks as if that's been the cause of all your trouble.'

'But it's not here now. Are you sure about this, Mr Barrett?'

I explained that unpleasant things had been going on in front of the picture and that it was saturated with the evil thoughts of the persons who used it. It could effect anywhere that it was placed and anyone who came within its range. They said the husband had an erratic personality with a very strong temper which made me wonder if he had been dabbling in black magic himself. His wife felt uncomfortable and hinted that he might have given her the picture with an ulterior motive.

I had to stay in the room while my helpers purged it and cleaned it out and got rid of all the evil influences. Eventually the oppressive atmosphere lifted and we all found ourselves sighing with relief.

But no sooner had we come out on to the landing than the stepson and the grandmother felt something holding them back at the top of the stairs. The boy looked at me.

'I can still feel it. It's still here!'

The only thing I could think of doing then was to relax and let Spirit deal with it again. My helpers brought in a man who had died in the house before the grandmother had gone to live there. He had had a heart attack on the top landing and fallen down the stairs. Every time he saw people on the landing he was trying to stop them from falling and in doing so he was stopping them from going past him. There was nothing to worry about, he was a good person, always willing to help and not wanting to hinder.

I had to tell him straight to mind his own business and to leave people alone because he was hindering them. He said he understood, but that he had another reason for being so protective. He was fond of the people in the house and he didn't want them to go into the boxroom either. He did his best to keep the door shut so that they couldn't go within range of the evil picture and he had continued to do this even when the picture left the house because of the influence which had still remained. I thanked him for all he had done and assured him that everything was all right now.

Dogs are able to pick up higher vibrations and this makes them very psychic, so I was pleased to see them running throughout the whole house wagging their tails. The stepson went upstairs to the toilet on his own and came back with a smile. The house was clear at last.

I still had to deal with the picture and I told them we would have to go back to the young woman's house again to see what was happening. It was quite late by then, but I think they all felt as eager as I was to clear up the mystery and my suggestion met with unanimous agreement.

There was just enough moonlight to see by as we made our way to the back of the building and came into the garden. We could hear noises coming from the shed where the picture had been put. We stopped in our tracks to listen and the old woman held on to my arm.

Her daughter whispered: 'What is it, Mr Barrett?'

'It's the picture. The best thing you can do is burn it!'

'I'm not going to touch it,' she said. 'If he wants it, he can have it back. I'm not going to be the one to destroy it.'

'Well,' I said, 'you're going to destroy yourselves if you stay within reach of it because it's evil.'

I advised her to make a decision about it as soon as possible and we went indoors. I told them I needed to stay in the house all night and they agreed to sit up with me so we made ourselves comfortable in the living room.

I sat with the little girl on my lap. Although it wasn't that hot, she was soon soaking wet with perspiration. Every now and then I had to comfort her and tell her to relax and that everything was all right. She was feeling the evil around us and the influence was trying to get through to her. Eventually she did relax and her mother put her on the settee and she went into a deep sleep. The older boy also dropped off, something he had not done until after four o'clock in the morning.

All I was doing was being quiet and calm, relaxed and reassuring them every time they wondered if something was going to happen. I was a channel for Spirit because Spirit has to have physical energy to fight physical things. When there is evil present, the energy force is a physical one, a human one. I have never known any evil to come from Spirit.

We heard only one brief noise. It came from upstairs and it sounded like a door being shut, whereupon the dogs got up and went running out into the hall, then up the stairs and through the house. They came back panting and wagging their tails again.

I hadn't ever come across anything as powerfully negative as the influence of that picture and I wanted them to understand why. So before I left I explained how places and objects absorb the vibrations of whatever takes place in their vicinity. If a picture is on the wall during a Devil's circle or any other evil or unpleasant happening, it will absorb and keep that influence and so will the walls of the room or building. Unless they are purged of all evil, anyone who comes near such influences will pick them up and absorb them without even knowing. They will then have a detrimental effect on that person.

As could be seen with the little girl, young children are particularly sensitive to higher vibrations because their psychic senses haven't yet been closed down as they are in the average adult. But once they become more involved with the adult world they realize that grown-ups are either totally unaware of psychic things or their disapproval takes forms ranging from lack of interest or disbelief to scorn or even anger. The little child who appears to have imaginary playmates is probably having fun with children in Spirit. Or they may sit happily while a departed relative tells them a story. Such experiences are so normal and so joyful that they seek to share them with those they love.

It is easy to understand the hurt and confusion caused by the adult admonition: 'Don't be silly. There's nobody there!' In order to survive in the world of adults then, children soon learn to keep such things to themselves. They may even be forced to the conclusion that they cannot trust their own senses and their own judgement because the adults they depend on provide no confirmation for this. Thus, the self-confidence of a sensitive child may be insidiously undermined. The psychic faculty must be shut off in order to be denied and after six years of age they may no longer be as sensitive until many years later or indeed ever again. Others, in an unconscious effort to preserve this faculty, seek solace in a world of their own.

When I have been to homes where people were worried about uninvited guests, I have found more trouble with human beings than I have with Spirit. Negative thoughts build up all sorts of atmospheres. Most people have noticed, for example, the atmosphere in a room where people have been rowing. People often say 'You can cut it with a knife!' Such atmospheres can generate all sorts of harm in those who are sensitive to them and these are usually children. So if I am asked to go into a home where there are young children aged up to five or six, or again round about fourteen, I check to see if they are the ones who are being affected by a human atmosphere. If not then I move on to the uninvited spirit guests.

I have never met a ghost, but on a number of occasions I have met spirits, people who have passed over, who for various reasons have chosen to continue living on the earth plane. More often than not they choose to stay where they have previously spent some of their earthly life. But when they occupy the same rooms as the other residents of a house, the effects on the new residents may take many disconcerting forms.

The publisher Gail Rebuck had such a problem in her London home. When she and her husband, Philip, first bought the house they had no children and decided to leave the top floor undecorated. When their first child, Georgia, arrived the top two rooms were decorated to make a nursery and accommodation for a nanny.

For the first six months of her life, Georgia had a maternity nurse. When it was time for the nurse to leave she told Gail that she had been having nightmares in her room and had sensed a presence at the top of the house. Putting this down to an overactive imagination, Gail didn't take her complaints too seriously until Georgia's first nanny joined the household.

Nothing else happened until Gail and her husband went on holiday. On their return, the nanny picked them up at the airport and was soon telling them how unpleasant it had been without them. She hadn't been able to sleep in her bedroom because she felt a presence there. One day, as she was lifting Georgia out of her cot, she saw a shadowy figure in the doorway and thought it was Gail. Of course if couldn't be, Gail was on holiday. After this she was so scared that she spent the week sleeping on the sofa in the living room downstairs.

The two young women had never met each other, nor had they spoken together. There seemed to be a chilly atmosphere in Georgia's room and her parents became concerned. Philip was sceptical but agreed to Gail's suggestion that they should contact someone who could look into the problem. So I was asked to go up and see what I could do about the disturbing presence at the top of the house.

The evening I called, the nanny was given the night off so we had the full run of the rooms without any interference. We went into the nursery and made ourselves comfortable, and I relaxed.

My helpers took over then and spoke through me. They said that there was once a fireplace in the room which had since been removed. Sitting by this fireplace was an old man of about seventy who had been living there in spirit since 1910. Before that he had lived there in the flesh.

Unaware that he had passed over, he continued living in the top of the house and as far as he was concerned he was still in his physical body. People came and fed him, helped him to dress and cleaned him and gave him his pipe of tobacco. Everything was as normal and he was quite happy.

When we are in the spirit world, the power of the mind is so strong that we can live in any surroundings we choose. On that level of existence, whatever is created by thought can seem totally real. So when I told him that he had actually died, he wouldn't believe me at first because everything was carrying on as it always had done. For him, every day was the same day.

We talked to him and argued with him at some length, my helpers using my voice to convey the conversation to Gail and Philip. They sat listening and they both seemed quite comfortable and relaxed. My helpers showed themselves to him and explained the benefits of living in the spirit world and how much better off he would be. He found it difficult to come to terms with this and was afraid to give up what he already had. If there was nothing else, as he feared, then he would have lost it altogether.

So we put a proposition to him. He could go off to the spirit world with my helpers on the understanding that if he didn't like it he could come and live with me. I was quite happy to have him if that was what he wanted, but I preferred him to try the spirit world first. Finally he agreed to trust me and went off with my helpers.

I told Gail and Philip that the old man had now left the room. Philip had seen the whole exercise as somewhat of a charade and apparently said to himself that if the door that was open closed at this point, he would believe there was some truth in it. The door closed.

Three days later, I was lying in bed wondering whether to get up since it was so warm and cosy under the duvet, when I heard someone talking to me. I recognized the old man's voice again and in my mind I heard his words: 'You told me I could come and live with you if I didn't like it in Spirit, didn't you?'

'Well, yes, I did. What about it?' I asked.

'You don't renege on promises, do you?'

'No, I keep my promises.'

'Good, I'm pleased to hear that, but I thought I'd let you know I don't want to come and stay with you.'

'You don't?'

'No. I like it here, it's wonderful! Everything you told me is true. I can be two years old, I can be twenty years old, I can be any age I like. I can live how I like as well. I can live in a palace or I can live in a shack. I can sit by my fire and smoke my pipe if I want to. I'm free!'

I heard all this with some relief and found myself slipping a foot out of bed and wondering what it would have been like if the old fellow had moved in. Somewhere in my consciousness he had said goodbye, but it was a cold morning in Bristol and I needed a cup of tea.

The two old men I have mentioned are typical of those in Spirit who may be felt as presences in a house, usually an older house. They 'live' there, quite unaware of the disturbing effect they may be having on the present inhabitants. All too frequently they are described as 'ghosts', with all the negative connotations of haunting and horror which go with this.

The fear and terror that surround these phenomena are the result of not knowing the facts. Once people are given the chance to understand them, how and why they occur, much will have been done to sweep away the distortion of the truth which has been promulgated and encouraged over the centuries.

What seems significant to me is that if people are aware of spirit presences, in whatever way, they are sensing the energies of a higher vibration as well as the physical energies involved in such phenomena. It therefore shows that their psychic faculties have developed to this point of awareness, as in the case of the two young women mentioned above.

If we feel we are under attack from someone else's destructive thinking we can protect ourselves by erecting a mental barrier. This is done by simply affirming strongly: 'No, I'm not having that and whoever is sending it can have it back!' This is the mental power that I have acquired which enables me to enter a house full of unpleasant, even evil, vibrations and be safe, because I have the power of my own convictions. The greatest enemy of that strength is fear. Once I start to be afraid, I am allowing these vibrations in. The only way to heal such a place is by relaxing and projecting a different vibration. This may take a long time, but it can be done. If a person cannot deal with it themselves they should get somebody else with sufficient strength of character to do it for them.

The mind is the most powerful thing in the world and it is up to us to look after ourselves. We all have a guardian angel who protects us from any spiritual influences that we don't want, and their power is limitless. But the power of human beings to hurt each other by word or deed is not in the realm of our guardians. Spirits can only interfere in human affairs if called upon for help and if there is something they can do.

So our first duty is to be responsible for ourselves. We can control our own destructive thoughts and substitute positive, constructive thoughts. Or we can let them run riot and control us. It is much easier to hurt ourselves with our own thoughts than we might imagine. We can generate a pain where one didn't exist, we can build a small pain into a big one, we can detract from our own strength of purpose, there is no limit. And the more powerful our thought, the greater the result.

But the wonderful thing about mental power is that it can also be used to build ourselves up and to affect those around us positively. For instance, Tom is a friend I have known for many years. Life has to be a constant challenge to Tom and he tends to move from crisis to crisis. If he can see a better way of doing a job he will take on the boss and do his best to persuade the man to see his point of view. He will do this even to the point of getting sacked.

One day he came round to tell me about his new job in the inspection shop of a big factory. I said it sounded like a very good job and I was happy for him.

'But Den, I've got problems.'

'You've always got problems, what is it this time?'

He described his boss as a nervous and highly strung person who didn't trust the men and was always coming into the inspection shop to criticize and interfere. The men were getting jumpy and things had got to the point where they were waiting for something to go wrong every time he showed up.

'I can't stand it, Den. I'll have to leave.'

I told him he had a job that was too good to leave and he

FIVE

Going Public

When I started going to Spiritualist churches I asked my father what he thought about it.

'It's up to you, Den. Do what you like, as long as you don't get cranky over it. Keep your feet on the ground, that's what it's there for. And don't have too much of it. You can have spiritual indigestion as well as food indigestion.'

It was good advice. Whenever someone becomes interested in a religion or anything spiritual, it seems the urge is to become involved in it as completely as possible, as soon as possible, to the exclusion of everything else in their life.

As I sat in the services I began to discover my own clairvoyance. I would take out a piece of paper or the back of an envelope and start scribbling. Things would come into my mind like 'Your mother wants you to know that she's happy and everything is going well' or 'Don't worry about your son, he's going to be OK.' I didn't know what it was for, I just felt I had to write it down. Then I would find myself going up to a complete stranger afterwards to show them my scribble. More often than not they understood the message and were very grateful.

It was not long before this ability was recognized, just as the healing was, and I was asked to take services as a medium myself. These invitations increased until my spare time was fully booked up for six years. I didn't have a weekend or an evening off. I began to feel that I was more in the world of Spirit than I was in the physical world. People told me how I talked about nothing else but 'the business'. They were right. I had nothing else to say. In my eagerness to please I had fallen into the trap my old dad had warned me about and I recalled his advice to keep my feet on the ground.

So I cut back on the church services and devoted more time to my healing work. This gave me the freedom to enjoy my physical life and as a result I found myself a more balanced person. I try not to 'get cranky' and develop a feeling of superiority. There are temptations, especially when patients shower you with gratitude. I like to think of myself as a genuine, down-to-earth person and I have found that this is what people respond to.

Today I will agree to take a service if a medium is unwell or the church has been unable to fill a booking. But, unlike some mediums, I refuse to commit my diary to months or even years ahead. This policy still takes me all round Bristol and the West Country and as far as South Wales. Services are fun because you never know who is going to come through from the world of Spirit. Some people's loved ones are real characters and of course they express themselves in just the same way as when they were on the earth plane. Sometimes a spirit helper or higher entity wishes to say something and their words can be very inspiring. So even those who have not received a message will feel that they have gained something from the meeting. This is undoubtedly one of the attractions of a Spiritualist service. I know that my helpers will try to bring laughter to the meeting because this relaxes people and raises the vibrations. This is essential, for most congregations will include those who are new, bereaved or in some kind of trouble.

People ask me what they can expect at a Spiritualist meeting. I explain that singing has the same function as laughter so it has a place in the service. It is essential to open and close in prayer so that the link with Spirit and the God force is made. Finally, it is the medium's job, through their psychic faculties, such as clairvoyance, to give the proof of survival. Living is a continuous process of learning and evolution and this life here is but a very small part of it. Contrary to popular belief, we do not contact the spirits, they contact us when we make ourselves available and tune in to them. We certainly do not contact the 'dead', those who have passed over, or indeed bring them back. We don't need to. They are so eager to tell their loved ones they are still alive and to give them proof of this and it is a sadness to them that there are not enough mediums to go round.

So the medium's job is a joyful one and very often an amusing one. I was down in Plymouth two years ago, taking a service. There was a big congregation and everything was going well. My clairvoyance was good and my helpers were coming through loud and clear. I came to a woman in the congregation and told her I had a woman with me who wanted to be recognized by her. Now I am what is known as a 'mental' medium, which means that I do not 'see' the person in Spirit, but my helpers describe them as if I can. They take over my person and my voice. I am conscious of what is coming through so that if anybody asks me anything about it I can verify what they say. But I am not aware of what I am going to say next. My spirit helpers told me that the woman I had come to needed plenty of proof so they set to work to give a detailed description of the person who was with her. I described the woman's age group, her build and her way of dressing.

Then I got to the necklace she was wearing and I described this almost bead by bead. I said: 'She tells me she's proud of her beauties.' Whereupon the congregation erupted into laughter. The woman smiled broadly along with the rest of them and it was a few moments before I could continue. Even the chairwoman beside me was chuckling. The woman accepted that it was her mother and her mother was able to give her a moving message of love and comfort.

When I sat down, I asked the chairwoman why there had been so much laughter earlier on about the necklace.

'When we say "her beauties" down here, we're not talking about "her necklace",' she said. 'We're talking about *these*!' And she cupped her hands under her bosom. No wonder my words had prompted such laughter.

The woman came up to me after the service. 'I hope you weren't embarrassed by what my mother said, Mr Barrett, but that was the first time I have been able to believe she was actually with me. So many mediums have come down here saying "Your mother's with you", with very little proof. It's a fair gamble that a woman of my age may have a mother in the world of Spirit, so I was never very impressed.'

I asked why her mother had mentioned her 'beauties'. She laughed and said it was the one phrase that had convinced her. Apparently her mother had always had a marvellous figure and she used to spend quite a time standing in front of the mirror, looking at herself from all angles and adjusting her clothes, especially around her bust. Seeing this, she would accuse her mother of being vain. Her mother would inevitably reply: 'What's the matter with you, I'm proud of my beauties!'

'They were the exact words I've heard my mother say so many times. I could see her there, pulling at her dress so it showed up the shape of her boobs!'

Driving home that night, I couldn't stop smiling. The spirits had known I wouldn't stand in front of a congregation and say: 'I've got a woman here and she's proud of her bosom!', but they found the best way round it.

I like to keep in touch with what is going on around the world in the fields of healing and clairvoyance and I have many contacts abroad. In 1975 I attended the annual congress of the International Spiritualist Federation which was held at Froebel College in London. The congress lasted a week and included seminars and demonstrations, followed by discussions on the various topics which had been covered. But I particularly enjoyed the informal meetings among the participants. These gave me a chance to talk to mediums and healers and to meet ordinary folk from all over the world.

That year there was a family from Iceland who were doing most of the serving at our table. One of the women was particularly striking, tall and statuesque like a Greek goddess. As she passed down our loaded plates, I said to her: 'You make a good mother.'

Her sister laughed. 'She ought to, she's got six children. There's the youngest over there,' she said, pointing to a boy of nineteen. 'Can you guess how old she is? She's younger than me and I am sixty.'

'She looks about thirty to me,' I said.

'She's fifty-four.'

This little conversation broke the ice and we soon became good friends. I had been doing some healing in my spare time so I wasn't surprised when the Greek goddess came and asked if I would help her older sister with a problem. Assuming it was a health problem, I said yes, and she took me over to their room.

Her sister was sitting on her bed clutching a small statue. Her hand was trembling and she was upset and tearful.

'Give her a bit of tender loving care,' I said, 'that's what she needs. But I'll do what I can. What's the problem?'

The younger sister said that they had wanted to buy her a present so they went out and bought a statue in a local antique shop. When she unwrapped it and looked at it, she went into a state of shock and became ill. The shock had brought on a period, yet she was a woman of sixty who had already gone through the menopause. Since it had happened as soon as she held the statue, they asked me if I would psychometrize it to see if I could pick up anything from it.

Psychometry had played a big part in my psychic development. It was one of the first methods I used and it works very well for most beginners. It involves sensing and interpreting the energies that an object has absorbed from the people or circumstances with which it has been in contact. Usually this is done by holding the object.

At first the older sister was reluctant to let go of the statue, even though it was the cause of her distress. I told her I had come to help and she put it into my hands. It was a simple painted metal statue of a person, the kind that is often seen on a mantelpiece. I relaxed and let Spirit come through to tell the story of the statue.

It had belonged to a woman at the turn of the century. When she had got married she had been very disappointed and heartbroken because she could not have children. Then she became pregnant and on the day that the boy child was born her husband had given her the statue to mark the event. He was their only child and the statue stood in the nursery while he was growing up. During the First World War he was called up into the army and she put the statue in her room. He was lost in battle and the inevitable telegram arrived saying that he was missing, presumed dead. In her grief she seized the statue and threw it on the floor where it broke in two. The husband found the pieces and mended it and it was put on one side. The war finally ended and prisoners were repatriated. One day a man turned up on their doorstep. He was badly scarred and injured. It was their son. The mother went into a state of shock which brought on a hemorrhage, the first period she had had for years. Her husband rushed to find the statue and put it back where it had always been.

When I finished the story I opened my eyes. The older sister was laughing and crying at the same time, but she seemed very happy. Now *she* had a story to tell. She was married and had an only son. There had been much disruption and unhappiness in the home and he had run away and never come back. She had always hoped that somewhere he was alive, but she never heard anything. She said her story was so similar and the woman in it had also had the period before the statue was back in place.

'Does that mean my son will be coming back also?'

'I haven't got a clue,' I said, 'but I'd like to think so.'

We looked closely at the statue again and found the join. It had been so expertly mended that it was virtually invisible. She said the great shame and heartbreak she had felt after her son's departure had disappeared at last and the release of her feelings had been the best tonic she could have had.

I never heard whether the boy did come back, but I always think that no news is good news. I know that Spirit found a wonderful way of healing her and something tells me that he did.

A few years later at a similar congress I became very close to another Icelandic family. The mother had one very short leg and her hip was deformed so that she walked with a limp. She used a stick to get around and I met her trying to make her way down a flight of stairs. I remarked on how painful her condition looked. She said that nego- tiating a staircase was the most painful thing of all and could I give her any healing?

I went back to her room with her and she introduced me to her husband and daughter who seemed to be a young woman of about twenty. Two days after the healing, she stopped using her stick and in another two days she started to dance with her husband in the evening. Her deformity was hardly noticeable. Then her husband asked if I would help their daughter. Although she had the body of a twenty-year-old woman, she hadn't matured mentally and was more like an eight-year-old child in this respect.

Acting on inspiration, I said: 'Yes, of course, but if I'm going to work on her I want you to make sure her hair is washed before I touch her.'

I thought it seemed a strange thing to say myself, but they agreed, probably thinking it was a necessary pre- liminary to the treatment. I told them I would call in an hour. So the mother went off to see that her daughter's hair was washed and I stayed talking to the father. He seemed a very strong and gentle man, very fond of his family. Almost to the second he looked down at his watch and said: 'Right, Mr Barrett. If you're ready, we'll go.'

Their daughter was sitting up in bed wearing a bed- jacket over her nightdress. As we entered the room both she and her mother were laughing at us. I went over to her and put my hand on her head. Her hair was still damp. I smiled at her. 'You know what I'm going to do, don't you? I'm going to see if I can help you to grow up.'

She grinned back at me. She didn't understand much English, but I spoke as clearly as I could. Instead of inter- preting, her mother said: 'Before you go any further, I have to tell you both something. For the first time in her life our daughter has washed her own hair, without being told and without any help from me. She had washed it just before I got here!'

The family send me a card from time to time. They tell me that the young woman has since grown up and married and now has children of her own.

It was a beautiful illustration of how the spirits are aware and listening as soon as their help is sought. Once the healer agrees to help, they go into action even before we make contact with the patient. Because I know this to be so, I have got into the habit of saying yes to whatever life offers me, confident that things will always work out.

So when somebody telephoned me in 1985, saying they wanted to come and see me about a programme they were going to produce on BBC TV, I said yes. I gave them an appointment and Michael York arrived with his secretary. They wanted to make a series of programmes about alternative medicine and they were wondering if they could talk to me about spirit healing. We had a good chat and after about an hour Michael York stood up and said: 'Well, I'll have to go back and throw all my notes away and start again after what I've just heard from you. But thanks very much, I've enjoyed it!'

Shortly afterwards he rang up and asked if I would be interested in appearing on the programme. If I agreed he would like to bring a film crew down to Bristol and film me healing. I agreed, but said that I didn't want him filming one of my patients. As a rule they were unknown to me and I didn't want them to arrive to find they were going to be filmed. He would have to provide the patient.

'That's quite OK,' he said. 'We've got a patient here.'

That was fine so I made an appointment for them to come at four-thirty on a Tuesday afternoon. I would be at a guild meeting between three and four o'clock, giving me plenty of time to get ready for the film crew.

On the day, the crew arrived at four instead of four thirty, bringing with them a female patient. I was the only healer at the guild meeting and there were a number of patients to see. I gave the crew the key to my flat and told should look after it.

'What am I going to do about *him*?'

I said: 'Think pink.'

Tom did a double-take. 'Think pink! What good will that do?'

I explained that colour has vibration and vibration has energy and the colour pink has a very soothing effect on the nerves. It is the energy of love.

'How do I do it?' he asked.

'Find an image of something pink like a flower or a spot-light, anything you like. Every time you think of him, whether you're with him or not, surround him with pink. It'll do the trick. In other words, project love towards him.'

'Love him!' he cried. 'How can I love him?'

'Well, give it a try. You *will* change him and you'll still have your job.'

Tom said he would have a go because he knew me. A few months later he told me about a conversation he had had with a workmate regarding their boss.

His friend said: 'I don't know what's happened to him, Tom. Hasn't he changed? Before you came here, he was a real pain in the neck. Now he's different altogether. He comes in and chats about the weather, chats about the football and cricket. He's never been like that in all the years I've known him. What have you done to him, Tom? Did you wave a magic wand or something?'

Tom said: 'You wouldn't believe me if I told you.'

How could he have told him that in his imagination the boss was walking around covered with pink roses?

'I did what you told me, Den. Think pink!'

them to let themselves in and make themselves comfortable. Meanwhile Michael stayed with me and watched me working on the patients. Spirit seemed to deal with them in no time and when I got back to the flat it was exactly four-thirty. I just had time to wash my hands.

They set up their cameras and the filming began. The woman got up on the treatment couch and said: 'Do you want me to say anything. Do you want me to say what's wrong with me?'

I said: 'Don't tell them anything unless you want to. I'd rather you didn't say what's wrong with you.'

I sensed that she had a serious complaint and treated her accordingly, giving a little running commentary as I did so. When I had finished we sat down together and I chatted to her for a few minutes. This was also put on tape.

Then the cameraman came up and said: 'I'm sorry, Dennis, we've put the wrong filters in and nothing has come out. I'm afraid we'll have to shoot it again. Can you do it again?'

'Of course I can. Spirit can do anything.' I turned to the patient. 'Do you mind if we do it again?'

'Not at all. I'd like that very much.'

So we started again. This time the take was all right. Fortunately the interview had come out the first time so they were quite happy. Before they left, the woman told me that the second healing had been more powerful than the first and that she had really enjoyed the whole experience.

Before the programme* went out, Michael rang up to tell me the date and time of the broadcast. 'I'd like to read you some of the script, I'm not sure if you'll find it satisfactory. It says: "Mr Barrett is a Bristol healer shown here working on a patient who has scar tissue on the left side of the abdomen." What about that?'

'That sounds fine.'

'Well, I didn't know whether you wanted me to tell them that you've cured the woman of cancer.'

---

* *The Healing Arts*, BBC TV, 1985

'No thanks! I don't want to be snowed under with patients. I don't want people to think I can cure cancer. It's not true. I work on the person, not the condition, and there can be many reasons why a person cannot get better.'

So the broadcast went out without mentioning the cancer or the fact that she had been healed.

Soon after I received about thirty letters from people who had written to me, care of the BBC. Besides these, hundreds were sent to the National Federation of Spiritual Healers and other groups, asking to be put in touch with a healer in their locality. The curious thing about the letters I received was that several of them said: 'I saw you on television healing someone who had cancer.' This was not mentioned at any stage, neither in the introduction nor during the programme, but they had picked up that the woman had cancer. The second curious thing was that many of them were desperately ill and had noticed an improvement after watching the programme.

The running commentary I had given was not as detailed as it would have been at a public demonstration where I describe what I am actually doing. It had not occurred to me that the broadcast was exactly that – I had given a demonstration before a public of millions.

It is the spirits' ability to use me in a totally natural way that makes my job so easy and so exciting. It means I can go into any situation with complete confidence even though I may be feeling nervous about my own abilities. When I give a healing demonstration in public I must not only be sure that they can work under such conditions, but that they will also be able to describe what they are doing in a way that will be understandable and interesting for the audience.

This is a new aspect of my work which I have enjoyed developing. I welcome the presence of other healers or clairvoyants who can not only corroborate what is going on, but greatly enhance the energy level available. I always begin a session by telling the audience that they all have a part to play and that they will be working too. By this I mean that they will be making a contribution to the total energy level. This they can do by relaxing and sending up their thoughts of love to the front where the healing is taking place.

Over the years I have found out who my spirit helpers are, but it is wonderful when someone comes up at the end of a healing demonstration and describes what they have seen.

My healing guide or main helper is a Red Indian of the Sioux tribe called Black Hawk. He wears a full headdress of blue-black feathers and was the son of a chief. He was only twenty-eight when he passed over. When I am working, I have given him full power to allow only the right and best help to come through so that he appears to act as a kind of doorkeeper. Mediums have seen him operating in this way during public demonstrations. When spirit helpers are queuing up to work on my patients, it is he who chooses the one who can best do the job.

I am often asked why there are so many Red Indian spirit helpers. Their way of living close to nature and spiritual things for thousands of years has made them wonderful natural healers and there is still so much that we can learn from them regarding this. It has been the wish of many of them, on passing over, to carry on their work on the earth plane as a loving service to humanity. This is the motivation of all spirit helpers who have been fitted by their experience in past lives to carry on their work through human instruments on the earth plane. (More about this in Chapter Seven.)

I have a Chinese doctor who uses vibrations of a very physical nature, almost manhandling his patients, although none of them seem to mind. I have known him lift up a man of two hundred and ten pounds to give him healing. I may put my hand on a patient when he is working, and it appears to be still, yet the patient can feel a strong vibration coming from it. He is able to help people with many different kinds of internal complaint. When he first came into my life he was identified by a medium while I was working on her friend.

The medium was Marcia Cuff, a psychic artist living

here in Bristol, who is able to draw or paint those whom she sees in Spirit. She decided to go home and paint the doctor the same day. As she sat down to work, he came and stood by her easel so that she could use him as a model. The following week she brought me the picture and I put it on the wall above my treatment couch. I asked him his name at that time, but he preferred to remain nameless.

However, in March 1989, Marcia took her portrait of the nameless Chinaman home to see if anything more would come of it. He came through in a 'circle' and also appeared in her studio again. He said he wanted the readers of this book to know more about him. His name is Ho Yang Sen. He used to teach the poor how to read and write in his village in Tianjin province where he was also a healer, using herbs and roots. He is able to apply healing to the nerve ends and his main work is to heal through the nervous system.

Mfollo the Zulu, was one of the first of my helpers to come through in the early days (as mentioned in Chapter Three). He is very physical and strong and makes great use of his hands.

There is also Kitan, a Tibetan lama who knows a great deal about herbs and homeopathy and was a very good natural healer in his own right. He was a librarian in a monastery and looked after the scrolls. Using his mental power, he was able to open up the body and work on the inside of a human being or a plant in this way. He proved that the mind is as strong and as sharp as a scalpel and much more effective.

And of course there is the Honorable Chang. Each of my helpers utilizes particular forms of healing, but I should stress that they are only the frontline of a limitless source of spirit help which is available to me.

During a healing demonstration the spirits describe what they are doing as they work through me. They can also say what effect their work will have on the patient and how they will probably react. Sometimes a patient has been misinformed about their condition and my spirit helpers are able to help here. After consulting their doctors, patients have found my helpers were right. As in my private work, I check that a doctor has been consulted so that their progress may be monitored.

Some healers apparently specialize – for example, in the treatment of nervous disorders or back trouble. I have not found this necessary because Spirit has proved that the power is available to cure any condition. I take the patients as they come and treat each one as an individual, for even if they say they have the same complaint the treatment may be different depending on the root cause.

I can expect to be confronted with any number of complaints. At a session in Cardiff in 1988, for example, I saw nine patients in the space of an hour seeking help with arthritis of the neck, arthritic shoulders, pain below the thyroid gland, tinnitus (ringing in the ears) and sinus trouble, the effects of nervous breakdown, epilepsy and bursitis of the elbow (inflammation of the fluid around the joint). As the session proceeded, I told the audience about my travels in America where I had begun to encourage others to join in. I was impressed to do the same in Cardiff and one young woman who came out for healing ended up helping me too and feeling the energy flowing through her own hands. She had not realized she had the healing gift, but my helpers encouraged her to have a go and find out for herself.

The healing demonstration has brought healing out of the private healing practice or clinic and in front of the public. It provides a platform from where I can explain healing in simple terms at the same time as I am demonstrating it. Perhaps most importantly, it makes healing more accessible to those in need. For some people it may be their first healing experience or chance to find out what it is all about. Others, like the young woman in Cardiff, may discover that they are healers too.

The whole theme of my public work is accessibility. I want people to become aware of the vast potential which lies untapped within them, to encourage discussion and to answer questions.

SIX

The American Experience

'Would you see a friend of ours who is over here from
Hollywood, Dennis? I've told her about you and she'd like
to see you while she's in England. The problem is . . .'

As the voice on the telephone went on to tell me about
her, the thought came into my mind – if there is a job to be
done and you are the one to do it Spirit will make sure you
get it. If the call comes you can say yes because you know
you can trust your spirit helpers. It is this 'yes' which sets
things in motion and allows them to work. This is the process for anything connected with healing and you can be
sure that your life will be enriched in a way you could not
have imagined.

This enrichment has become more obvious to me with
hindsight. When the call comes I am simply concerned
with the patient and I agree to help as much as I can. I am
not interested in what the job will lead to. In this case, a
short telephone conversation with my friend Oliver Caldecott set in motion a chain of events which was to lead to a
high point in my life and also in my work as a healer.

Ruth had been talking with Oliver and Moyra about
Moyra's healing and this had inspired her request to come
and see me. People contact me from all parts of the
country. They frequently recommend their family, friends
and business associates to come here if they are ill so I am
not surprised by the interesting mixture of patients from
all walks of life who end up on my healing couch.

Ruth came down to Bristol for treatment and during the
healing I felt there would be some improvement which

she would notice as the days went by. We talked together for a while before she went back to her London hotel.

On her return to California, her friends wanted to know what had happened because she looked more upright and yet her condition had been getting worse over the years. She told them she had had spirit healing and they said: 'How do we get to see this healer, how can we experience it for ourselves?' They discussed the cost of air fares and hotel accommodation and it was obviously impractical for all of them to come over to England. So they came up with the idea of clubbing together and paying for me to go over and stay in their homes as a guest. Even with a generous allowance this would still be a considerably cheaper and more practical solution.

It was April 1985 and I had been made redundant from work so I was free to say yes. The idea was for me to go over for a week to see the small group of twelve people who had agreed to cover my expenses. I was to stay with Ruth, she would drive me around and act as chaperone with the patients.

When I arrived in San Francisco, Ruth told me the group had grown somewhat and I was due to see thirty-six patients in four different areas of California during my one week's stay. She had rented a log cabin at Big Sur. We drove down through groves of beautiful coast redwoods. The cabin was perched high on the side of a valley in the rugged Santa Lucia mountains.

I live in a flat on the north side of Bristol. The window of my healing room looks out on to a small lawned garden and, apart from this, I see little of nature. During the drive from the airport I began to realize the vast scale of everything in the United States. Now, as I stood outside the cabin and gazed out over the expanse of the blue Pacific Ocean, being close to such a beautiful part of this planet, I suddenly felt immersed in the glory of nature. The sense of freedom was overwhelming and I wanted to breathe it in through every pore.

Before I flew over, I had asked Ruth to send me case histories of all the patients. I said they could be as long or as short as they liked, and I ended up with a sheaf of letters, some of which amounted to eight pages. To wade through all this was quite a chore, but I read each one carefully and then put them to one side. I knew it would be impossible for me to remember all the details, but this wasn't important.

When I did eventually see them, I asked them to lie down and relax and tell me about themselves and their problem and many of them would say: 'Well, quite honestly there's nothing much wrong with me now.' It came to me that their letter had been their prayer to the God force and as soon as they sent such a prayer they started feeling the benefit. Spirit was able to work as soon as they had expressed their needs via the healer. The same happens when people ring me up. They start getting better before they come here because they have linked up with the source of healing, the God force within.

I like the idea of writing things down as a way of handing it over as a prayer to God. Often, if you just write what you feel, things can come out which you didn't know were there. This is good therapy. Expression in all things – release of emotion and relief from its effects – is good medicine.

Nine patients were due on each of the following two days. They came from all over America, some of them travelling all day and all night. They were friendly and very interested in how healing worked. I find this wherever I go. People want to know what is going on, how it works and why, just as much as they want to have their aches and pains put right. When they realize it is not a question of faith or any mumbo jumbo, but the operation of natural law, they become even more interested. (In the next chapter, I shall explain exactly how and why spirit healing works.)

We drove from Big Sur down to Berkeley, to spend the next two days with Debra and George near the University of California. Here, the patients were lively and inquiring, very much like the atmosphere on the campus.

I recall one young man in particular who was very bewildered and didn't know what was happening to him although he had been meditating regularly. After all, he said, meditation was supposed to be good for you. He had come for healing because he felt drained of energy and generally out of sorts. My helpers came through and revealed that he was psychically open, so I taught him how to relax and settle down to meditate and how to switch off afterwards. This is very important. Meditation or concentration on a spiritual subject for any length of time opens the psychic energy centres. If we don't switch off afterwards, energy can drain away from these opened centres. Secondly, negative or harmful vibrations can be absorbed through the same open centres. The mental act of closing in prayer automatically closes the centres so that the full benefit of the meditation is retained without any debilitating side effects.

Each patient seemed so eager and curious I could have spent three hours with them instead of the one hour they had been allotted.

Soon it was time to say goodbye to our hosts Debra and George and make the six-hour drive north to Arcata on the Californian coast. We took Highway 101 for some time when Ruth turned off onto a road running parallel which wound through groves of giant redwood trees. She slowed down and opened the sun roof. I couldn't hear a sound, not even the engine.

Ruth watched me through her sunglasses. 'Well, Dennis, what do you make of this, then?'

I described the great peace I could feel in the area.

'Ah, so you can feel it too. This is a sacred burial ground of the Indians. Even long-distance truckers slow down and go through holding their breath. They never drive through in a hurry or sounding their horns.'

The majestic redwoods inspired humility. Ruth told me that the Indians not only had forty separate memorial groves in the region, they also regard the trees themselves as great spirits with whom they can communicate.

As if a reminder were necessary to jolt me back into the modern world, a sheriff's car pulled out in front of us and escorted us for thirty miles at exactly one mile an hour below the speed limit. Arcata is another beautiful place by the sea, though again, I had little chance to take in my surroundings. Mellie and Tom were open-hearted hosts whose co-operation made it possible for me to work at a high energy level. We saw twelve more patients in less than two days and it seemed that we had hardly arrived before it was time to make the long drive back to San Francisco in the early hours of the morning.

The thirty-six patients we had seen had a variety of problems, including chronic arthritis, heart disease and nausea, but there was no one whom we couldn't help. The whole visit had been such a success, the group decided to organize a second healing trip lasting two to three weeks round Thanksgiving the same year. I was quite happy about this. I had enjoyed introducing them to Spirit and I could now look forward to seeing the result of the treatments.

I hadn't been home long before feedback in the form of telephone calls and letters began to arrive. Some simply thanked me and Spirit for coming into their lives while others gave detailed descriptions of the progress of their healing. A man who had had a heart condition for the whole of his life couldn't believe that it was nearly gone. Ruth told me that 'as it improves he is amazed to find how his thinking must change to that of a healthy person without a heart condition'. Mellie wrote to say that she had been healing people with her hands and that she could physically see the difference afterwards. 'When I am in the process, I feel like I am with God,' she said. 'I don't feel like I do it – but I do feel like I aid in the realignment.'

I couldn't have described the experience of healing better myself. This letter was the first hint of things to come and it pointed the way towards one of the most important results of my trips to the USA.

On my second trip, just before Thanksgiving, I was due to start work in Seattle and spend the third week holidaying at the home of a Hollywood film star. But because of the bad weather in Seattle, we decided to postpone my work there and concentrate on the two groups of friends near San Francisco, at Carmel and Berkeley, and a third group at Arcata up near the Oregon border. This meant that I had to cancel the holiday. I wasn't disappointed about this because I was going over to do a job not to have a vacation.

I have often thought about it because one thing leads to another, and I have sometimes wondered who I might have met in Hollywood and whether I might have been able to help some of the other personalities who work there. I knew that for some reason it was not to be since I was prevented from going there. It was not the right time for me to meet the stars for that would have taken me in a different direction.

During the first US trip Ruth had been my chaperone. But early in November she was writing that there would be no need of one anymore because there had been so many requests to work with me at each location. People who had experienced healing the previous spring now wanted to be linked with the healing of others and they wanted to be known as 'apprentices' rather than 'chaperones'. By the time I arrived at the end of November, the requests to take an active part had grown considerably. Ruth had had to use her organizational skills to the full.

'I'm snowed under with apprentices,' she wrote. 'I've had to ration them to four hours each.'

I assured her that we would cope quite well in the usual way. I was so pleased to think they were feeling open enough to have a go and let Spirit work through them.

What I did was ask them to assist. If I had a patient I wanted to reassure, for example, I might say to the apprentice: 'Come and hold his hands while I work on his neck.' One would start with me at nine in the morning, then another would take over after lunch, and so on through the day. Every one of them said the same thing – 'If anybody lets you down, give me a call and I'll be over straight away!'

In the evening the group of friends I was staying with would all gather round and we would have a session where they would take it in turns to work on each other. So there might be up to six people working on one patient. In this way they all experienced the sensation of being used properly. It wasn't a question of just going through the motions. They would get confirmation of this from the patient through comments like 'Whoever has their hands on my knee, it feels great!' or 'I can feel something happening underneath your hands on my chest there – the left one is more effective than the right one', as the case may be.

Seeing the effects of people being drawn into the healing, I began to think it would be a good idea to involve others, as I believe everybody has the potential to heal. Spirit is everywhere, healing is everywhere, and the God force is within everybody so we can use it wherever we are. The thing that prevents people from working is doubt. They think they are not capable and they have all the hang-ups which are ingrained in us from childhood. They think that healing is only relevant to a particular personality. We have to realize that we all have the whole energy force of the universe at our fingertips. The only limitation is that which our mind puts upon it. I began to see the proof of this when my American friends wholeheartedly said yes.

Although I can recall each treatment at each location, certain patients come to mind more easily because of the unusual circumstances involved. At Berkeley a young woman in her early twenties came in and I was immediately struck by the intense emanations coming from her. During the healing session a picture fell off the wall with quite a bang. My spirit helpers reassured everyone and told them not to be apprehensive. The young woman was able to absorb large amounts of energy and was an absolute powerhouse. Because she was not using it in a constructive way she was experiencing various forms of discomfort. She also periodically gave off sufficient amounts of energy to create disturbing effects around herself such as the falling picture. She would need further guidance in ways of channelling the energy she was so easily absorbing.

After her, a couple came in. The young man was twenty-two. His girlfriend spoke up for him and described a situation which didn't make much sense to me. He was

94

having bad nightmares and couldn't sleep. During the day he was in a very upset state and couldn't relax. He felt his life was in turmoil. When she had finished talking about him she said she would like some healing herself. I told her we would tackle the young man first.

He got up on the treatment couch and lay there as stiff as a board, his face tense and the knuckles white on his clenched fists. It is impossible to get through if the patient is not relaxed and this is one of the first things a healer must ensure. So I said to him: 'Tighten up as much as you can. Tense your muscles, then take a deep breath and hold it. When you let your breath out, relax completely. Let it all go.'

These, I discovered, were the wrong words to have said because he belonged to a group who believe in letting it all go in a certain way. They go out into the forest and into the glades and have a screaming session which may last for days – a real hysterical release. So when I uttered the magic words 'Let it all go!', he started. He screamed and shouted at the top of his voice. I was a bit shaken and didn't quite know what to do. Thank goodness the next patient was not due for another hour. This was hardly a good advertisement for painless healing!

So I said: 'Come on Spirit, you've got a job here!' and did the only thing I could think of. I relaxed completely and just kept my hands in contact with his forehead. Spirit took over and let him go on ranting and raving. It felt as if he had been rehearsing this event all his life. I thought, they're happy, I'm happy. My assistant, Debra, seemed happy, so I just let it all happen.

'Oh, my God! Oh, God! . . .' he screamed and yelled incoherently.

After about twenty minutes of this the spirits said: 'Right, time to stop!'

And he stopped, just as if a switch inside him had been turned off. Apparently this was fine because it was all part of the formula he was used to. Many American therapists work to a timetable. You have an hour in which to express yourself and when the hour is up it is time to stop. So he switched off.

95

Once the noise had died down, Spirit wanted him comforted first of all, so I put my arms around his shoulders and held him. He stopped crying then and said: 'I'm so scared.'

'What are you scared of?'

'I've done some terrible things, horrible things.'

'What have you done?'

'I've made living sacrifices. I've eaten living hearts. I can't go on with the thought that I'm so evil!'

After some more of these kinds of confessions, the girl butted in to say that they had been involved with a woman who had used regression in hypnotherapy to take people back into their past lives. She had taken him back a number of incarnations to a time when he was the altar boy at a high priest's sacrifice. It was his job to make sure the knife was sharp. And when the priest said 'Strike!' he struck. He had to lunge down into the chest of the live victim and carve out the heart. Lifting it on high, he would take the first mouthful of the bloody flesh.

It was obvious to me that the person who had regressed him had dabbled. People who use this kind of therapy have got to know what they are doing and dabblers don't. Hypnotism is one of the most wonderful therapies as long as it is used properly. If she had taken him back into the past, sorted out what his hang-ups were and then shut the door – in other words made sure that he left it all behind as we do when we are reincarnated – she would have been doing a good job. But she had told him to come back before she had stopped it welling up into his conscious memory, and this was the cause of his nightmares.

My first reaction, before Spirit could say anything, was: 'Go back to the woman who hypnotized you and tell her you want her to shut the door.'

'I won't go near her again,' he said. 'I'm too scared she'll do me even more harm.'

At this my helpers regressed him completely, back to a time when he was a slave in an ancient Egyptian household, around the time of Moses. Then they took him forward a little to the time of the living sacrifices and began to instruct him. This was one of his biggest trials. He had overcome it and it was all over. His previous lifetimes were all separate and must be kept separate. Now he could move on to his next lifetime, and the next. They showed him how he was continually going through stages of development, how he had progressed and improved in every lifetime and now he had come to the time in the present when he had to be clear of all bad memories. The doors to these must be shut and never opened again.

In over twenty years of work I have only been involved in such a deep hypnosis three times. I can't hypnotize people myself, but my helpers can when they come through. When they had finished they told him to remain lying down and relaxed and to stay relaxed while we turned our attentions to his girlfriend.

She had a gynaecological problem so I asked Debra to help with it. We worked on her for half an hour and talked to her for another half hour and in all that time the young man never moved. I went over to him and asked him how he was.

'I'm fine.'

'If you want to get up now, you can,' I said. But I saw that he was moving like someone who was still hypnotized. I had to tell him to lie down again and deepen the hypnosis. I told him that nobody else was ever going to hypnotize him again, only me. So if I ever met him again, my helpers would be able to hypnotize him, but nobody else would be able to get through. It is essential in hypnotherapy to make sure that the patient will not ever respond to the same stimulus again; this effectively closes the door.

I heard later that the young man had slept well and was continuing to do so. There had also been a marked improvement in his relationship.

For the final week of the trip I flew up to Seattle to meet the last group of patients who had been organized by a Japanese woman, Okomo. Some of the apprentices came with me to enlarge their experience. I stayed with Sadie and Bill and after the first day of working they took me out to a Japanese restaurant. Here I was introduced to the delights of Japanese-style prawns. These are king-size prawns fried very crisp with a tasty sauce.

The next day Okomo said she was going to take me out for a meal and asked where I would like to go. I said I had enjoyed Japanese food so much I would like to try it again. So she took me to her favourite restaurant and we dined in style. This time the prawns were fried in a crisp, fluffy batter. Okomo noticed me enjoying them and I said I would like to take some home, but I had eaten them all. I knew it was the custom in the States to take the leftovers home in a doggy bag. In some places they gave you a little lunch basket which you could take out on a picnic.

Okomo called the Japanese waitress over and explained that I was a newcomer to the States and that I had appreciated their Japanese prawns and I would like some more to take home with me. She smiled broadly at me and went away. When we came to pay the bill, a great big man, the size of a Sumo wrestler, came up with a box in his hand. It was beautifully tied up in the Japanese way. He bowed to me and offered me the box. Okomo explained that he was overwhelmed at being able to give it to us.

'How much is this?' I asked. Perhaps the price would be overwhelming too.

'Oh no,' said Okomo. 'You have done them an honour by asking to have some more. If you had wanted them on your plate they'd have filled it up ten times!'

When we got home and looked in the box there must have been at least ten good helpings of those wonderful prawns.

Bill is in the publishing business and on my last day in Seattle I saw a lawyer friend of his who came for healing. The lawyer was engaged in defending a man whom he felt was unjustly accused of murder. He found many of the details of the case bewildering and he had reached a point where he didn't know how to proceed for the best. During his healing session the spirits brought up the case because it was weighing on his mind so much. They pointed him in the right direction and he was happy with the new line of approach. He felt he would now be able to save the man's life.

After the healing, he and Bill got talking and came up with the idea of starting a healing centre. If I was prepared to come and live in the States, the lawyer would deal with all the immigration papers and work permits. They offered to pay for an office and all the equipment I might need and the means of running the centre as a business. They talked of several alternative propositions.

'You could settle over here and live and work here entirely. This would enable you to travel throughout the United States. Or you could spend part of your time here and the rest of the year in Britain. You could make a lot of money, Dennis. Which idea do you like best?'

'I don't like any of them. I'm happy as I am. I can see no good reason for leaving England. So that's my answer gentlemen.'

Perhaps they were surprised at my decision but, when the question of money comes up it embarrasses me. People ask me about my fees and I tell them that I have no fees. The gift of healing is a complete gift from Spirit. It came overnight and it costs me nothing. Money is just a means to an end. As long as I have enough to cover my expenses I am quite happy. I do not want for anything so I can't ask people who may be short of money to pay for what I enjoy doing.

What price can be put on healing? I think of the woman who could not be touched and wonder how much it is worth for her to be able to have her husband put his arms around her again. I think of Ruth who could go back to the States and put on a swimming costume for the first time in years – and now goes swimming every day. She couldn't walk very far before she came to see me. How much could I charge? There is no limit to what Spirit can do, but I can't put a value on it because it is beyond price.

Somebody once heard me expounding this point of view about healing and fees and said to me: 'I think you're being selfish, Dennis. All you want to do is give, yet you won't allow anyone else the pleasure of giving. Apart from goods, money may be all someone can give you as a token of gratitude.' I could see the point, so now I do accept freewill donations. I reserve the right to spend the money on anything I like. For instance, I have a large telephone bill. Or if a patient comes along who is not very active I might want to order them a taxi home.

I got back to England by mid-December when the feedback from the second trip began arriving. Mellie wrote from Arcata to say that their healing group was working well along the lines I had suggested. They talked with patients after the sessions and then had a get together among themselves to share thoughts and make notes. 'Again, thank you for sharing with us,' she said. 'I feel like one of the ripples that goes out when a pebble is tossed in a quiet pool of water.'

Another ripple from the pebble came from a woman in Newport, Oregon, who had started putting her hands on patients, saying: 'I've felt Spirit working through me.'

Dawn Overeem also wrote from Arcata to thank me for the healing she had received and 'the opportunity you gave me to work with you apprenticing that last morning. It has truly changed my life.'

By the middle of 1986 healing groups had been set up in Berkeley, Arcata and San Francisco in California, and in Seattle, Washington. They were carrying on and expanding the work we began there together. If they have any problems or there is something they want to know, they just ring me up.

One of the groups heard of a woman in Oregon who had been ill for a long time. She had cancer which was causing her a lot of suffering. Her husband had given up an executive job in the city to buy a farm. They kept sheep and had been trying to make a living from them. Katie spun her own wool and wove things out of it to sell. They used wood for heating and had to pump their own water.

The group asked me if I could help her. I explained how I work in such circumstances and that I wouldn't make promises I couldn't keep. If she was as bad as they said, the only thing I could do would be to ease her passing.

They had been told that Katie didn't have long to live, but the hospital couldn't say how long. Ed was in financial trouble and he didn't know if he could afford to keep her in hospital much longer or whether he could afford to do anything else. The cost of hospitalization was so high that they thought it was a better proposition to pay my expenses to fly out there and do what I could than to keep her in the hospital.

Then someone offered to arrange an Indian healing ceremony. The Indians had only recently extended this to include the average white American and, knowing their reputation as healers, Ed was eager to let Katie take part in one. All this information had been relayed by a friend of theirs, Ellen, who lives in Fairfax, California. 'Would the healing ceremony clash with my own work?' she wondered. I said no and that it would be fine. She said that in that case Ed would find out if he could cover the expenses and ring to let me know the outcome.

In the very early hours of Tuesday morning Ed rang to tell me it was all arranged. There was a ticket waiting for me at Heathrow to be picked up at eleven that morning. So the call had come to go to the other side of the United States and, apart from the air ticket, I had only fifteen pounds in cash. But I knew that if I was needed, Spirit would find a way of getting me there, otherwise the call wouldn't have come. I had always said I was ready to get up and go at a moment's notice. Now I was actually going to do it. I had a few hours to pack and get to London and at 12.45 p.m. I caught a plane to San Francisco where I would be met by Ellen who would put me on the plane for Portland, Oregon.

'Let me get this straight, Mr Barrett. You want to enter the United States of America with a one-way ticket, only fifteen pounds in sterling, you don't know where you're going and you don't know where you're staying?'

The woman on the San Francisco immigration desk looked at me with incredulity. 'Do you expect me to believe this?'

'Yes. There's my ticket. I've told you the story.'

'It's a one-way ticket, Mr Barrett. You need a return ticket. Who is the person you're going to stay with?'

'His name's Ed.'

'Ed! Are you crazy? Just how are you intending to get

101

there – even though you don't know where it is?'

'There's a lady waiting for me outside now. She's going to give me a ticket for Portland and tell me who is going to meet me there.'

'Have you got any money other than your thirty dollars?'

'No.'

'But it will cost you much more than that to get back to England. Do you have any credit cards?'

'None that are valid over here.'

'I'm sorry, Mr Barrett. I can't let you through. You'll have to wait over there while I send for the inspector.'

It was some time before the inspector arrived. 'I'm sorry to have kept you, Dr Barrett. I've just had a message to expedite your passage.'

'I'm not *Dr* Barrett, I'm Dennis Barrett.'

'Pardon me. Are you a doctor? Are you Dr Barrett?'

'No, I'm not a doctor, I'm Dennis Barrett. I'm a spirit healer and that's what I'm here for, to do some healing.'

'Well, I don't get this. We've got a message here saying a Dr Barrett is coming through and we want to get him through quickly. If you had said you *were* Dr Barrett, you would have been straight through.'

'What, even if I didn't have a return ticket?'

The inspector pushed a hand across his forehead. 'I doubt if we would have thought of that.'

'Well, I'm sorry. They didn't have any right to tell you I was a doctor, because I can't claim to be one. But I've been here before, you've probably got a record of me somewhere.'

This seemed to bring some relief and he went to check the records. When he found I had already entered the country twice before and gone back again he felt a lot happier. He told me that what had clinched it was the fact that I wouldn't call myself a doctor. I had to spend another half hour talking about spirit healing and he became more and more interested and quite reluctant to say goodbye. Finally he let me go through.

'I'm fascinated by this subject,' he said. 'I wish we had more time to discuss it. But let me know how it goes.'

I had been kept three hours. Poor Ellen was heavily pregnant and on the point of collapse from waiting for so long. So I told her to give me the ticket for Portland and point me towards the right door.

I went on through with another one-way ticket, knowing I had to meet someone called Ed at the other end. I got off the plane feeling quite confident that everything would be all right and as I was walking down the first corridor, a man stepped in front of me and said: 'You must be Dennis.'

'Yes, that's right.'

He held out his hand. 'My name's Ed. When Ellen rang me she said to look for the biggest man on the plane – you sure as hell are him!'

It was late in the evening when we set off in Ed's truck for the farmstead where I met his two daughters. We were due to go to the hospital the next morning to see his wife. Katie was acutely ill and she couldn't eat or remain comfortable for more than a few moments. Ed warned me to expect to find her in a very poor condition.

Her bones showed through her transparent skin and she was suffering great pain. Although she was drowsy from the effects of the drugs, she was very pleasant and seemed pleased to see me. I marvelled at the quality of the hospital facilities. The standard of care was very high, but unfortunately so was the cost of it. I sat next to her, talking to her, giving her strength, soothing her. This is what I do in these kind of situations, giving reassurance and keeping contact by holding the hand. When the patient is drifting, as she was, a firm grip gives the necessary reassurance.

At about six o'clock the nurses got her dressed and we took her by car to the house where the healing ceremony was to take place. The house and grounds were luxurious. The lawn of about half an acre was surrounded by mature trees and in the middle of it was a wooden pavilion. Here we made Katie comfortable on a couch where she could rest until it was time for the ceremony to begin. We went indoors to talk with friends and have a snack. After this we went outside to relax on blankets and groundsheets to await the arrival of the Indians who were due at dusk, around nine o'clock.

Meanwhile the women carried on with the preparations. They had been occupied with them for most of that day, in particular making ready the tobacco ties. These were made by tying wisps of tobacco into little pieces of cotton which were in turn tied to a very long length of string. The effect was like the rag tails on an old-fashioned kite. There seemed to be miles of them wrapped round a big stick. This was the first preparation.

Next, the whole of the inside of the pavilion was blacked out; every crack and crevice was filled so that not a chink of light was visible. Then they went round with smouldering sagebrush wafting the smoke into every part of the room.

I was lazing on the grass watching all this from across the lawn, aware that I was being severely bitten by midges. When I saw the women coming towards us with smoking sagebrush I assumed it was to bring us some relief, but it was part of the preliminaries. We had to stand up and be smudged, as they called it, all over. Up the trouser leg, under the arms, everywhere. This was an essential purification to prepare us, as well as the building, for the healing ceremony. It was a relief to move about. I had only been sticking it because the others were. I asked them how they had managed to lie there being bitten to death without complaining.

'We were only sticking it because you were, Dennis!'

None of the women were allowed into the ceremony if they were mooning (menstruating). The Indians maintained that during this time acids are released from the woman's body, through the skin as well as in the menses, and these will adversely affect the carefully controlled conditions. Menstruation also changes the vibrations given off by a woman so that on both counts she cannot be allowed to take part in any religious ceremony. The women were disappointed, but they respected the rule. So a few of them stayed behind when we went into the pavilion.

It had been dark for two hours when the Indians arrived

in big American cars. My first glimpse of them showed me people who bore themselves with dignity, their flowing black hair setting off their colourful dress. Ten Indians accompanied the medicine man who led the way to the pavilion, and we followed them in. They stood in the centre of the room and watched us in silence as we arranged ourselves on the floor with our backs against the wall. They waited for the room to grow quiet before they put down a patterned blanket in the middle of the floor and set five white tins around its edges, each filled with earth. Poles were put in the tins with banners tied to them. They were made from different coloured scarves with a red banner set at the northern corner. The medicine man sat on the blanket and the length of tobacco tie was tightly wound from pole to pole to make a kind of enclosure around him. The pavilion had become a sacred place.

There were thirty to forty people in the room. Katie was on the couch with her family around her. She seemed to be holding her own very well. The Indians checked that all the ties were in place and the equipment was ready, including the drum. The medicine man addressed the gathering and said: 'We are going to pray now. Do not be alarmed if the grandfathers and grandmothers come in and if the animal spirits come in and crawl over your legs. All will be well.'

Then the lights went out. It was the blackest place I had ever been in. Out of the darkness came the voice of the medicine man. He outlined what was going to happen in his own language, then explained what he had been saying in English. The drum began to beat with a slow steady rhythm. The Indians broke into a chant, then the medicine man said a prayer. This pattern was repeated again and again to the beat of the drum. I felt as if my own heart had taken up the same rhythm. Soon every heart in the room would be beating in unison. We were becoming centred in readiness for the main part of the ceremony.

Suddenly there was silence, the chanting was over. And there beside him stood a tall Indian chief, dressed in full regalia. It was his spirit guide, my helpers were telling me and they went on to describe him. He had a headdress of eagle feathers. Ornaments of white fur and feathers hung around his ears and his face was marked with bands of white and yellow. Around his neck hung a breastplate interwoven with turquoise, red and white beads. He had come to oversee the activities and decide which spirits would be allowed through. The ceremony continued with the medicine man saying: 'Now we will pray.'

The praying began with the patient herself who said thank you for everybody's love and then she went on to say that she wanted her family to be looked after and she wanted everybody to be happy. This was followed by a prayer from everyone else in the room in turn. The prayers were mainly for help and healing – the whole theme was healing – and there were a few other people they were also concerned about. There was some impassioned prayer going on and by the time my turn came, I was so choked with emotion I could hardly get the words out. Round the room it went as the energy seemed to build and build. It was over an hour before the last prayer had been offered up. The medicine man did some more chanting and talked to us for a few moments before he said his final prayer. There was a short silence and the lights went on again.

One of the Indians turned to me and said: 'This is worse than a sweat lodge.* I've never known it as powerful as this!' I realized that I too was bathed in sweat. My shirt was saturated as if I had been out in a thunderstorm. When my spirit helpers are working through me they generate a great amount of heat; I noticed that everyone seemed drenched in the same way and kept quiet.

In the centre of the room the tobacco ties were no longer round the poles. Somehow they had been rolled up into a gigantic ball. The ball was tossed around so that we could examine it. My Indian friend said: 'That's a tight one,

---

* A small, low domed tent (*ini tipi*) used by North American Indians for prayer and making contact with the Great Spirit. Once the entrance is sealed, water is splashed on to the hot stones in the centre to create a steamy, sauna-like atmosphere.

that's good!' Apparently it was a mark of honour to get a very tight one. The tighter the ball the more work has been done by the healing spirits. I couldn't find a loose end on the ball. There was no way that I could see how a human hand could have rolled it up so meticulously.

The ceremony had lasted three hours and the Indians were as pleased as we were. They all spoke of the power that was present which had been greater than in any sweat lodge. I looked at Katie. She seemed to be thriving. She had looked good at the start, but I had put that down to excitement. I would have expected a person who was dying of cancer to be dehydrated and worn out by the heat, but she was glowing with strength.

We made our way into the house where a buffet meal had been laid out. In the hospital, Katie hadn't been able to keep her food down. Now she ate like a horse, clearing everything that was put in front of her. Eventually it was time to leave for Ed's place and we fell into bed around dawn.

I slept fitfully, my mind still going back to the ceremony. It was the most fantastic therapy I had ever experienced. To me, the most remarkable and rewarding thing about it was the emotional release. If we could help people to let go like that, we could help to cure cancer and other stress-related illnesses, help them to pass over, help them to feel better. If people are uptight, as we all are, and they go into an emotionally charged atmosphere like that, they can enjoy the benefit of releasing their pent-up feelings.

Katie stayed awake for most of the next day and I spent a good deal of time talking with her and her family about life after death. She was so relaxed, and though she felt a little nausea, her suffering was nothing like it had been before.

Ed had managed to get some plane tickets for Friday morning and we set off in his truck for the airport. Everywhere we went seemed like an airport and it was not until Ed dropped me off that I realized we had been driving round and round the same airport. He didn't want to stop talking about Spirit and the things that went on in the spirit world and it was his way of keeping me with him until the very last minute. Finally we were shaking hands again. He promised to let me know how they were all getting on once I had got back to Bristol. And I saw in his eyes that we both knew the next chapter in the story.

As they were checking my documents at Portland, I asked the receptionist to get in touch with the inspector at San Francisco to tell him I was on my way.

'That's what I've just done on the keyboard, Mr Barrett, and your name's come out at the top of the list.'

Ed got home to find Katie in a coma from which she never woke up. She had passed peacefully. He told the girls who were nine and ten that now they would need someone to help out in the house. Nonsense, they said, that's what they intended to do from now on.

As I put the phone down, I thought of the first time I had heard his voice just a week before. I thought I was responding to a single call for help then, but it had come from the whole family. My role had been supportive, strengthening and reassuring throughout. My main purpose had been to help Ed and the girls to let Katie go, because they didn't think they could cope without her. The spirits had got the job done. They had proved that they could get me anywhere that I was needed, no matter what the obstacles might be. They had also given me the privilege of actually seeing the Indians operating as healers. In a profoundly moving experience, I had been part of the spiritual linking of two cultures.

Every time I went to the States I always stayed with groups of friends who called themselves 'The Family'. They did everything together and worked and played harmoniously. The group at San Francisco was based at Woodacre and consisted of four couples. Among the four couples were Marc and Ane Takaha. Marc is a third-generation Japanese American, a very talented and compassionate man. A year after my visit to Oregon, the Takahas invited me to spend a few weeks with them at Woodacre. We could get together in the usual way, have some healing sessions and catch up on the news of all the groups. So in May 1987 I was lucky enough to find myself at San Francisco airport again and this time I had a return ticket.

Set into the hillside, their wooden bungalow was surrounded by beautiful trees with the roof nestling among the branches. Deer roamed freely, visiting the garden by day, so that Marc had to put a high fence round his vegetable patch. As I entered their home I realized that it was a very special place and felt privileged to share it. He and Ane slept out in the garden so that I could use their king-size waterbed. Their attitude was typical of the hospitality I found everywhere in America. Whatever I needed was supplied.

Like so many things in the States, the waterbed was a new experience for me. If I coughed I found that the bed went on shaking for some minutes afterwards. And this experience was followed the next day by the Japanese hot tub. This is a large wooden tub filled with very hot water and is used as a form of communal bath. Some people stay in it for half an hour, but I found ten minutes in that heat quite sufficient.

Like so many people in California, Marc was full of interesting ideas. I was looking out of the window one day and saw him sitting cross-legged in the middle of the vegetables. He seemed to be crooning softly to himself. I asked Ane what he was doing.

'He's singing to the plants. It's part of our approach to growing. We talk to them too. It seems to encourage them to produce their best.'

Ane explained that their approach to gardening is to regard all things as part of a living whole, which naturally includes the earth and the plants which grow in it. The planet too is regarded as a living being. This biodynamic approach takes organic growing a stage further in suggesting that there is a spiritual dimension to plants and the soil which must be given equal consideration. Ane and Marc lived according to their ideals and it was a pleasure for them to help others and to pass on the benefits of their own experience. They tried to be at one with their environment, giving something back to it as well as taking what they needed. The peace and serenity which resulted from this attitude permeated the house.

Marc enjoyed cooking. He said it gave him a chance to do something for others and I asked him what he meant by this.

'It's a chance to give someone your love without them realizing. First it's put into the food. Then some more goes into the preparation. Then you enjoy eating it with other people. By the way, Dennis, it's your turn for some healing!'

This time *I* was the patient and the group worked on me. As part of the healing the six of them sang to me for a couple of hours. This was their way of relaxing me and allowing the healing energy of love to be directed to me in the form of song. I knew it was also one of the most effective ways of raising the vibrations. That is why singing features so prominently in Spiritualist services. So they had a singsong with me on this occasion. I felt wonderful. To round it off we went out to a restaurant.

While our order was being taken, Debra began to tease us about reading our palms. She took my hand in hers and pretended to read my fortune and tell me about myself. When the waiter saw this he held out is hand. 'Do mine, please!'

Debra laughed. 'Oh, no. I'm not the one for this. He's the one you want to see.' And she pointed at me.

So he turned to me and asked me to do it. I said I was not a palm reader, but as I said it I realized I was a medium and a medium is never off duty. Perhaps there was a need here.

'I don't do tricks like that, but I can tell you a little about yourself.' And I did tune in and told him how unhappy his childhood had been, but that now he was coming into his own. I also saw a wedding in the near future. He went away beaming, to return a moment later with the next course.

'By the way, sir, you were right. My young lady is the waitress here.'

'Bring her over then.'

He not only brought his girlfriend over, but most of the restaurant staff came too. They stood in front of me and I told them both about the joys of living and the joys of being happy together and that they would be together forever if they wanted it. Then I joined their hands as if I was marrying them and said 'God bless you'. And with that we went on with our meal.

When we were leaving, the young man was waiting for me at the door. 'I wanted to thank you. We're getting married in a few months and we needed to know what you had to tell us. We will never forget it, I promise you.'

Ane tells me that every time she goes to that restaurant the waiter says: 'We're happy, we're happy. You tell him we're happy!'

I would like to think that, if nothing else, I have left my American friends happy. So many of them came to understand and accept that they were spiritual beings and the consequences of this fact. This is what made sense to them and this is what brought them joy and happiness. It was as if they had been waiting for something which they could have described in many different ways. But a demonstration of healing allowed the penny to drop, as what I was saying took place before their own eyes and they could feel it in their own bodies. This only happened because they were ready – it was what they had been waiting for.

It might be suggested that America offered me fame and fortune and I had said no to both. But I sought neither of these; I didn't go there for myself. America has given me the chance to do something far more important. I have been able to reach a cross-section of people and show them Spirit in action. They took part and felt the energy of the God force flow through them. This convinced them to go further and do it themselves to help others.

One of my patients, who has since become a healer herself, had said two years before that she felt like 'one of the ripples that goes out when a pebble is tossed in a quiet pool of water'. I was the pebble, tossed by Spirit into that pool of waiting water. The ripples move ever outwards because the world is ready. It is hungry for the truth.

In the 1960s and '70s people talked of peace and love,

and thought the only way to find this was to opt out. But fulfilment is found by 'hanging in', by giving back. This is what the healing groups in America have found and the feedback I get from them is a testimony to this. I am so thrilled when I hear of their adventures with Spirit and their successes. Typical of these is the letter Debra wrote to me in November 1987. In it she tells how a woman of thirty-five came to her for healing. The doctors had said she must have her breast removed because of a tumour. 'We worked with the healing spirits of love and the lump disappeared – that very day!'

Her letter goes on to show how she exemplifies everybody else who has discovered their inner truth: 'When my heart is open and I forget everything except loving the patient, there is the energy. I feel that the most important thing I've learned from you is that healing really has nothing to do with technique, but has everything to do with loving the patient and helping them to relax and be healed.'

In just a few words she managed to sum up the experience of so many who have aligned themselves with Spirit and linked up with the God force within.

SEVEN

How Healing Works

When a child once asked me what spirit healing was, my immediate response was that it was the energy or love from God used to heal people. She seemed content with that answer and didn't need me to go into any more detail. Patients often ask the same question, but they are not as easily satisfied, they want to know more. Sometimes they find it difficult to understand spirit healing because they are unable to grasp the concepts of the spiritual basis of the human form and the energies involved.

I begin by explaining that each of us is Spirit, a part of the God force, sent out on a journey of experience. There are numerous planes of existence of which life here on earth is only one. Each plane provides different environments, experiences and challenges. Spirit can experience any of these environments as long as it has a vehicle or body which is compatible with that environment. This ensures that Spirit has a 'skin' around it which is vibrating at the same rate as its surroundings.

The etheric plane is the nearest level of existence to the earth plane. Here, Spirit surrounds itself with an energy body known as the etheric body. It is this body which a spirit can use to make itself recognizable to us. Because it is vibrating at a much higher rate than the apparently solid forms of the earth plane, an etheric form cannot be seen with normal eyesight, but it *is* visible to clairvoyant vision.

When Spirit wishes to experience the earth plane, it must take on a further energy body in addition to the etheric. This is the physical body. Having two 'bodies' enables us to leave the physical and return to the etheric plane at will. This occurs for most of us, for example, during the sleep state, when we go 'astral travelling'.

In the same way, the God force as Spirit also takes on the forms of animal, vegetable and mineral. Just like human beings, each form has an etheric or energy counterpart which is its blueprint. Thus the blueprint for any physical body is contained within the etheric.

On the blueprint nothing is missing, damaged or diseased since these conditions are features of life only on the earth plane, not outside it. So, part of spirit healing involves the realignment of the physical body with its perfect etheric counterpart.

An etheric cord, linking the two bodies, extends from the back of the crown of the head from one to the other. Because of the shimmering appearance of this structure, it is known as the 'silver cord'. When Spirit gives up the physical body, as at the time of death or passing over, the silver cord is severed. During astral travelling (travel on planes outside that of the earth), the cord is capable of infinite extension.

Without the God force within which animates it, our physical body would be as lifeless as a discarded coat. As well as energy in the form of food, water and oxygen, it needs other vital energies which come from the sun and beyond the solar system. These energies are finer and are first absorbed via the etheric body. They enter the seven main openings on it which appear as bell-shaped structures connected at intervals to the physical spinal cord. The point at which they link with the spinal cord is known as an energy centre or *chakra* (the Sanskrit word for 'wheel', because ancient Indian mediums saw these centres as whirling wheel-like vortices of energy). They are situated at the base of the spine and in the regions of the spleen, solar plexus, heart, throat, brow and crown of the head. The finer energies are absorbed by the chakras, to be used in the etheric body and transmuted there for use in the physical.

It is at this point that many people suddenly lose interest in discovering how healing works. For others, whose eyes have not glazed over or widened in panic, I will go on to explain the energies. All energy emanates from its divine source and operates according to natural law. The energy used in spirit healing is a cosmic force vibrating at a much higher rate than physical energy. It must therefore be stepped down, like electricity going through a transformer, before it can be used in a physical situation. One of the functions of the healer is to act as the transformer. Spirit energy is directed towards the healer, enters via the etheric and passes out of the healer's hands in a form which can be used on the patient. If necessary, the etheric body of the patient may be used to screen off high-frequency energy which their physical body couldn't tolerate. This process is the operation of natural law by those who understand it (the spirits) through people who may or may not understand it but are willing to let it happen (the healers) for the benefit of the patient.

Because of the nature of the energy, which comes from outside me, I can work all day using my hands without feeling tired. It is often the case that I feel more energetic then when I started because I have received such an energy boost.

I feel the energy projected by Spirit in a number of ways – heat, cold, or vibrations and movements of various kinds. Most common of all is a tingling in the fingers and palms of my hands. The patient may be aware of different sensations. Quite often they are preceded by a sense of calm and relaxation. They may even feel drowsy. Those in Spirit who are working with me know what is needed and how to set up the appropriate conditions to bring about the best result.

Using spirit energy in this way is a skill of the highest order whereby the spirit operator must know how to control its frequency, intensity, direction, duration and practice. By the controlled use of vibration alone, Spirit can work on or inside the patient's body in a direct line with the healer's hand or away from that direct line. So, for example, the hands may be placed at the nape of the neck while tissue is removed from the front of the head.

A cooling vibration may be used to sedate or anaesthetize a part of the body which is receiving treatment. By increasing the vibration the area may be stimulated. Like a laser beam, energy can be focused to cut or to weld. The same beam can be diffused a little and used with a vaporizing effect to dissolve diseased or unwanted tissue.

What doctors and surgeons have only recently begun to do in hospitals with the latest equipment, Spirit has been doing through me for the past twenty years. Cateracts are removed with laser beams. Vibrations are used to break up kidney stones. Ultrasonic scans are made by putting instruments on the body to get a picture of what is going on inside. All of this the spirits can do. They can also heal inside the body using vibration. Scientists have discovered that vibration is infinitely adaptable and medicine is moving more and more towards the use of these techniques. In time it will be understood that we can use one piece of equipment to do it all, just by changing the wavelength.

Those in the caring professions, such as doctors, nurses, social workers, teachers and ministers, have a love of humanity and they all wish to serve. They do not change when they pass back into the etheric (the world of Spirit); their need to serve goes with them. So they are given the opportunity to carry on by being reincarnated and going through another lifetime of physical service. This means, however, that they will not be able to serve in this way until they have reached maturity and can take responsibility. The second option is to work as spirit helpers through 'instruments', as they call healers on the earth plane.

Once a person is back in the world of Spirit, they see that there are no barriers of race or creed, just one God from whom the energy of love emanates. They come to understand that this love is a universal energy force, not a human emotion.

So Spirit can work through anyone here on earth. The only criterion is that people on the earth plane attract people of like mind in Spirit. Like attracts like, honesty attracts honesty, directness attracts directness, physical attributes attract physical attributes. This ensures that there is harmony between healer and spirit. I am six foot two and weigh two hundred and forty pounds so my helpers tend to be large people with a firm nature. I have already mentioned Mfollo the Zulu, Kitan the Tibetan and the Chinese man who are all taller than I. Like many male healers, I also have female helpers working through me. They too tend to be large women and they may deal with gynaecological problems or manifest a more feminine approach to a patient when this is required. Many women healers will likewise have male spirit helpers.

People have asked me during services how their loved ones can come back in the etheric in a form which they can recognize. And on the same theme, why do spirit helpers appear as persons from a certain time or race? I remind them that, being the God force within, our subconscious mind is preserved when we pass back into the etheric world and this contains a complete record of our journey through life. It supplies the form of the etheric image which people sense when they 'see' Spirit. It would be pointless for them to appear to us as pure Spirit, so they come as a person with whom we can identify. In the case of the spirit helper, they will tend to adopt the external form which they had when they were last engaged in therapeutic work on the earth plane.

Spirit helpers who work with healers on a regular basis have great knowledge and experience covering a wide range of healing practice. Furthermore, they can call on specialists in any field of therapy, control them and guide them through the healer. This is why I maintain that we have unlimited resources and abilities. There is nothing a healer cannot do, provided they will do it. I know many wouldn't agree with me because we all have our barriers, but they are of our own making. If we say to a patient 'I'll try and ease the pain, if nothing else' we are in effect saying we don't think we can do anything else and that is all that gets done.

However many helpers there are, there is one who always directs the work. This is the healer's guide and teacher. The guide is a highly evolved being who has been given the special task of watching over, guiding, protecting and teaching someone, perhaps through many life-

117

times. I have often been faced with the reality though, that no matter how devoted the guide may be, they cannot interfere with our free will. The bond is based on a loving relationship in which two spirits agree to journey together.

One of the guide's functions is to bring in those who are best qualified to do the job and to exclude those who are not. My guide, Black Hawk (whom I mentioned in Chapter Five), knows I will only work with the best and he has ensured that this has always been the case during our long partnership. We are 'blood brothers' and have been together for many incarnations.

Practitioners in Spirit are eager to exercise their skills, in many cases treating a condition which would normally be considered inoperable. For example, few surgeons would tackle a brain tumour which extends down into the spinal cord. The spirit surgeon can not only operate and clear such a condition, but do so without any of the usual trauma involved. At its present stage of development the medical profession is unable to practise in the way that Spirit can, but once it demonstrates its readiness and sense of responsibility, the knowledge will be given.

People often ask how it is possible to tell whether a spirit guide or helper is of the highest quality. The spirits welcome this question and their answer has always been 'Judge us by our fruits'. My work with the spirits for over twenty years has given me complete confidence and trust in them. So when patients come to me, even if they seem to be beyond help, I know that my helpers have directed them because this is the right place and the right time for them to come.

There is a great need for instruments and my helpers assure me that for every healer there is a queue of willing workers in Spirit waiting to assist humanity. Healers tend to be used by Spirit as channels for healing energy though some are able to direct these energies consciously themselves. Any healer who has reached this stage of development will be taught how to do this by their guides.

Though I work from home, healers may be found in

clinics and centres, in churches and working alongside the medical profession. Some work in a team where one healer takes the lead while the others assist. Such assistance may take the form of directing energy towards the patient for use by Spirit, or in administering comfort and reassurance.

People have remarked that most of my patients are women and I would estimate that eighty per cent are. This is interesting because the different energy patterns of male and female create a polarity between them which can be used by Spirit to their benefit. Of course this does not mean that I cannot work just as effectively with male patients.

The interchange of energies is continually taking place between ourselves, the environment and all those we encounter, whether we are conscious of it or not. The more sensitive we are, the more aware we are of these exchanges and the effect they are having on us. As sensitivity increases, the psychic* senses (such as clairvoyance) come into play and we are aware of an even greater range of stimuli. We may, for example, be able to see the energy radiated by another person in the form of colour. The spirit body, the etheric and physical bodies all give off emanations, the physical emitting a force of the least intensity. These emanations of spirit energy appear to surround the person as a coloured glow or aura. Many healers have noticed changes in a patient's aura according to their different emotional, physiological or mental states.

Being sensitive means being aware of another's condition and our sensitivity may be such that we can take on that condition and know what it is like to experience it. This may be very useful in a healing situation, but when it hap-

---

* A 'psychic' sense enables us to be aware of certain very high-frequency vibrations or energy patterns at present undetected by physical science. The word 'psychic' is currently defined as meaning 'outside the possibilities of natural law' (*New Collins English Dictionary*). However this definition shows a lack of understanding of natural law since nothing can exist outside it.

pens without our realizing the results can be very unpleasant, as my friend Ken found out.

I go to Torbay every year with a Spiritualist group for a
week of lectures and to meet old friends and perhaps
make new ones. We have such a good time it is more like a
holiday. One year I was down there with Ken and his
family. We were about to sit down to tea when his wife
came up to me looking distressed. 'Ken's ill,' she said.
'Will you go and see him when you've had your meal?'

'Why, what's the matter with him?'

'I don't know, but he's in a terrible state.'

When I first knew Ken he suffered from very bad headaches. Spirit had removed an egg-sized growth from his
head and since then he had never suffered again. As I
made my way down to see him with his two daughters, I
wondered if the old condition had returned. The curtains
were drawn, just as if he had a bad migraine. One of the
girls put her finger to her mouth and whispered: 'Daddy's
not very well. Don't speak very loud.'

She was right. He looked at death's door. As I reached
out to put my hands on him, my helpers came through
and what they told me made me burst out laughing.
'There's nothing wrong with you except that you're pregnant and you're suffering from toxaemia!'

He shook his head and groaned, then suddenly sat up
in bed, swung his legs out and started walking about. 'I
don't believe it!' he said.

'I do. You've taken on someone else's condition.'

I asked Spirit to take it away and left them there to go
and get changed for the evening festivities.

I saw him later, sitting with a woman in the coffee bar.
He called me over. 'Den, come and meet Mrs Green, she's
got something to tell you.'

The story was that Mrs Green had telephoned her
daughter that morning. The young woman was pregnant
and frightened she might lose the baby because she was so
ill. She came back from the phone call, saw Ken and told
him about her daughter.

'I've had her on my mind continuously, yet I saw Ken
this morning and forgot all about my daughter after-

Early days. The healer in 1968.

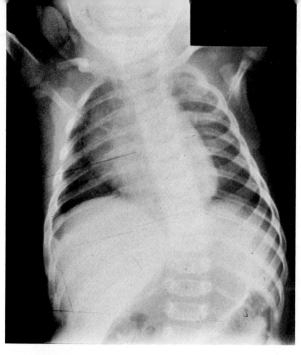

X-rays of Jody Alloway's spine taken in 1984, at 4 months (left), and after healing at 5 months (below), show her total recovery from infantile scoliosis.

'Jody has grown up to be a perfect little madam in every respect'.
(Olan Mills)

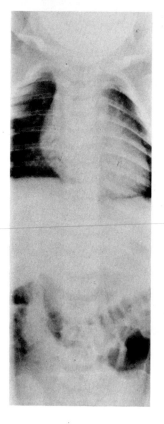

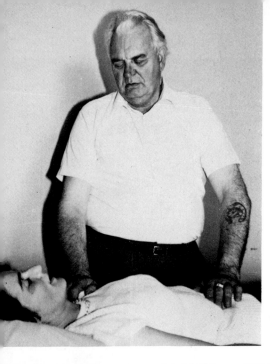

The first stage in healing involves restoring balance to the patient's energy centres. (Marion Peters)

The healer is directed to the area requiring treatment. More than one area may be treated at the same time. (Marion Peters)

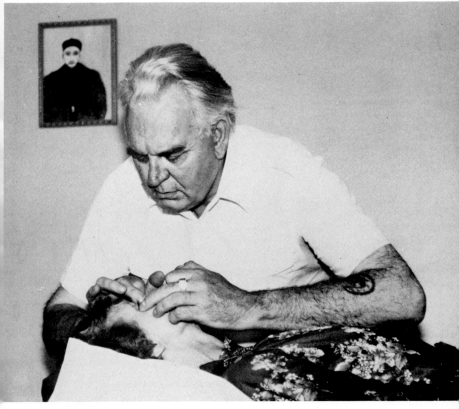

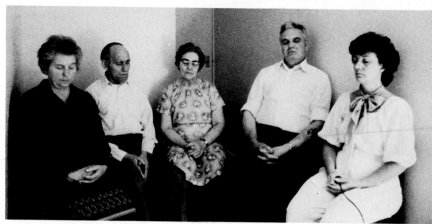

ABOVE *Dennis's wedding in 1949. His father, Edward, stands at his right. 'In later years I came to understand how much he taught me by playing the devil's advocate.'*

BELOW *Sitting in a 'circle' to develop psychic awareness. Dennis calls this 'having a party'.* (Marion Peters)

Take this hand,
this flesh,
this instrument
and mold
for me
one gesture,
perfect
and complete.

Bill Roepke's drawing of a pale blue alpine flower, found in the mountains near Prasanthi Nilayam, symbolizes the healer, Dennis, and his budding American apprentices. (Jack Angelo)

LEFT   *The leaf that materialized on the desk of London writer, Lucas Ralli, can only be found on trees in certain parts of India.* (Lucas Ralli)

ABOVE LEFT   *Dennis's spirit doctor, Ho Yang Sen, who appeared to psychic artist Marcia Cuff so that she could paint his portrait.* (Marion Peters)

ABOVE RIGHT   *Kitan, the Tibetan monk, was drawn by psychic artist Wilma Jillings in 1967 from an impression she received on holding a letter written by Dennis.* (Marion Peters)

Sai Baba's powerful gesture of greeting just before Dennis left India to return home.

wards.'

In the meantime Ken had taken the condition from the mother without realizing and felt very ill.

'As soon as Ken told me about this, I got on the phone to her again and my daughter said: "Mum, everything's all right. I feel wonderful!"'

People are becoming increasingly sensitive and these sorts of things are happening more and more. If we cannot understand why we feel unwell, but straight away send out a little prayer for whoever is really suffering in this way, we make an opening for Spirit to use our energies to help that person. However we cannot always be sure that we are dealing with conditions which are pertinent to that patient, because they could have picked up a condition from someone else. So if I am not sure I ask the patient if there is anyone they know who might have similar symptoms.

A woman came here recently from America saying she was completely depleted of energy. I couldn't find anything wrong with her and I didn't feel drawn to work on her. So we just sat and talked. During the course of conversation she mentioned a sick old lady whom she used to visit every day. She went on to describe the symptoms for this dependent woman which were the same as her own. She had been worrying about her and in doing so she was focusing on her without switching off.

When people complain of feeling out of sorts and low in energy for no apparent reason, rather than looking for signs of flu, I find myself drawn to put my hands over the patient's solar plexus and keep them there. This covers the solar plexus chakra to stop the drainage of emotional energy and to allow the patient to be topped back up.

It is the same situation as becoming open through healing, meditation, or any other kind of spiritual activity. We need to switch off or close down and the ideal way is to close in prayer. Another method I use with beginners is to ask them to picture their chakras like open lilies on a pond. To close down, simply fold the petals up. Soon they can be closed instantly by just the thought of doing so. It is essential for the healer to be able to switch on and switch off. Our first duty is to ourselves, for if we get depleted or sick we cease to be able to help others.

When we work with a patient we first have to switch on. This is the act of linking with or tuning in to Spirit and then the patient. An essential element in any spiritual activity is relaxation. We need to relax the body by letting go, and relax the mind by clearing it of as many thoughts and pressures as possible. The brain will gradually slip into an alpha rhythm state which is ideal for Spirit to work through.

When beginners start to work there is always the problem of responsibility. They wonder if they will do it correctly or if it is their fault when there are not immediate and spectacular results. This attitude prevents them from relaxing. What should be understood is that they are instruments. The final responsibility is not theirs but Spirit's. We have tuned in to Spirit, now we tune in to the patient.

The approach to the patient should be gentle and reassuring. We have to inspire confidence by our relaxed and positive demeanour and we must not offend, embarrass or hurt them. There is a strict code of ethics among healers which means that high standards of behaviour are adhered to. I have already mentioned that I prefer a chaperone to be present and I insist on this with female patients. The public can bear in mind that all registered healers are also fully insured.

I ask my patients to remove their coat so that they feel comfortable when they sit or lie down, but there is never any need to remove any clothing. Spirit can work through any material. Having encouraged them to relax as much as possible I ask them to tell me what is wrong because this allows the link between us to be strengthened.

As we meet on the same wavelength, we find we can pick up their conditions. In my case I get sympathy pains. If someone has a pain in the abdomen, I feel the same pain. If someone's back is bent with pain, so is mine. I may be feeling a pain in the neck when the patient is complaining of headaches. In such a case, this would tell me where the cause of the problem is and where to put my hands. As soon as I acknowledge these signals they disappear.

Of course I am only describing how *I* work. Every healer finds their own way because they are being taught by their own guide. This is why a spirit healer cannot be trained how to heal by outsiders alone. We can learn how to conduct ourselves properly and benefit from the experience of others, but ultimately it is going to be a partnership between healer and Spirit. A healer has to be a feeling person and no amount of training can give them a heart.

When we are drawn to put our hands on a part of the body, we are almost invariably held there by our own feelings. If we don't know the intricate details and workings of the physical body, Spirit does and will direct the energy from our hands to do the right job. I put my hands on the patient, but some healers prefer to hold them above or near the patient's body. My own experience is that the patient is reassured by physical contact, especially if they are feeling apprehensive about their first experience of spirit healing.

Spirit needs an empty mind to work through, not one cluttered up with decisions, problems and worries. If I stand over a patient and try to analyse what is happening and what is needed, I am defeating the object of the exercise which is a simple, loving, caring approach both to the patient and to the work.

We tune in by caring. No one can work on a patient for whom they have no feeling. It is impossible for a person who dislikes someone to tune in to their needs. There is no mystery about this. When we love or care or sympathize we send out an energy force which can link with another. When we feel hatred, dislike or indifference we prevent this link from being made. In a relationship the love link goes out from both partners and creates a strong energy bond. Feelings can be so mutual between a husband and wife, for example, that the man may get his wife's labour pains. Mental communication works in the same way between two people who love one another.

Every one of us is part of a universal energy force, the

God force within. Because that God force is submerged in the subconscious mind, we are not aware of the power we have within ourselves. But when we relax and go within, as we do in meditation, we are allowing ourselves to tap the universal energy source and at once we have a link with every entity in the world of Spirit, the force that they can contribute, and the force within every person we meet who is willing to meet us. This is why, once I have found my own balance of energy I can touch the energy level within the patient. This allows the God force within that patient to emerge and heal wherever healing is required.

While healing is taking place, Spirit encloses the patient and the healer in an energy shield. This has been seen by many members of the audience during healing demonstrations as a cocoon of bright light surrounding them. It demonstrates how important it is to preserve the flow of energy and protect it from outside interference. The healer must be able to work undisturbed, since any interruption can lead to a loss of energy flow between Spirit and healer and between healer and patient. There have been occasions when someone has come close to me and just said 'Excuse me' and I have felt an unpleasant vibration like an electric shock pass through my body. The effects of such a shock may last for some time. For this reason, if a patient comes to me with a chaperone or group of people, I explain to them that it is best if they don't talk to me during the healing session unless they have to. If they have to approach me they should make sure that they speak softly first before they touch.

I may spend a few minutes or up to an hour on a patient, depending on what is required. I encourage them to remain relaxed for a few moments afterwards, so we may sit and talk for a while before they are ready to leave. If I think another appointment is needed they may make a booking there and then. Sometimes the patient experiences drowsiness so I warn against driving until the feeling passes. This is another reason for having a chaperone.

When the question of payment arises, I explain that I don't charge a fee, but I will accept a donation if they feel they would like to make this gesture. I keep a little box in the healing room for this purpose. Some full-time healers with families to support are obliged to charge, but I am fortunate enough not to be in this position. I like to think that Spirit looks after me and I always find my needs are met adequately.

I am sometimes asked about children and animals. My experience is that parents don't seem to bring their children to visit healers. It is as if they feel that children shouldn't experience healing until they grow up. But they don't stop to think that Spirit is the same whether in the body of a child or an adult. The principles are the same and I welcome child patients. One of the accepted rules of healing is that children must be taken to a doctor first anyway. We work with the doctors and do not seek to countermand their treatment or advice to any patient, old or young. There has been an emphasis on the healing of adults – particularly 'hopeless' cases or the terminally ill – in the past, but this attitude is changing.

I would take the same position about a sick animal. Some healers specialize in the treatment of animals, often working closely with veterinary practitioners. Wherever there is Spirit, there is life. Healing is for all in the widest possible sense.

The question of relations affects healers in a personal way too. Many healers who feel too close to their own families to give them help have created a barrier of their own making. The same kind of barrier exists when they cannot give themselves healing. Yet all we are doing is linking up with the God force and it is this which does the work.

Once the healing session is over, the link between Spirit and the patient continues and the treatment is given for as long as is necessary. I need to break the link, however, so that I can dismiss the condition and deal with the next patient with whom a new link must be made. This may be done mentally, but it is very common for healers like myself to wash their hands with water to reinforce the mental action.

There are many cases when contact healing is not possible, either due to factors such as distance or mobility or the unfeasibility of it if, for example, the patient is violently unbalanced. In all these cases absent healing may be used. Just as in contact healing, the healer is the intermediary who makes the link between the patient and Spirit.

Some patients have a problem understanding how healing can still take place and be as effective at a distance, but this is because they don't appreciate the nature of the energies involved. Absent healing is not the power of thought, nor is it mental telepathy which uses physical energy. The power of communion with the God force is a spirit energy not a physical one. Furthermore, outside the earth plane distance and time are irrelevant.

When I receive a letter from any part of the world asking for help, the contact is made through the letter. Spirit can go back in time to the moment when the letter was being written and healing can begin then. It is not even necessary for me to ask for help. Similarly with telephone calls, the fact that I am willing to help means that those who work through me can link with the caller and help immediately starts to be given. The call for help is transmitted at a spiritual level by the God force within, whether it comes from the patient or the healer. Distance makes no difference to the amount of energy transmitted because it is unaffected by physical resistances. I am often told that the patient felt as much heat passing into them as if I had been physically present. There is no distance between the God force within me, within Spirit or within the patient.

Years ago, at the healing clinic, Maurice Flook told us how he was stopped in the street one day by a neighbour. She wanted to know if it was possible to give absent healing to somebody as far away as Australia. She felt that the other side of Bristol was probably far enough and perhaps after that the power would start dropping off.

Maurice's reaction was: 'What's the difference? Here or there, it's all the same to Spirit.'

So the woman showed him a letter from her daughter who was living in Australia and was not very well. Maurice asked for absent healing for the young woman when he got home.

A few days later he met the mother again. 'Have you heard from your daughter recently?' he asked.

'Not since that letter I showed you.'

'You know she's moved, don't you?'

'No, I didn't.'

'Oh, yes,' Maurice assured her, 'she's moved. But she's all right.'

'Well, that's news to me. I can't think why she should do that. Thanks for telling me. Perhaps I'll hear from her about it.'

She went away a little bemused, not knowing whether to believe Maurice or not. But soon she called to see Maurice with a letter from her daughter which he read with a smile.

'Dear Mum, notice the new address. Bill came home from work in the middle of the day full of excitement. "Pack a case," he said. "No need for anything else. We're moving to the other side of Australia. There's a plane waiting for us. We've got accommodation and everything is laid on. All you need are your clothes." Well, we left the house straight after I'd packed. Into the car, into the plane and flew right across Australia. We've settled in here really quickly. But such a funny thing happened to me. I hadn't been in the new house very long when I had a dream or woke up, I don't know which. A man was in the bedroom. He was about five foot four, a young fifty . . . He told me not to be frightened because you had sent him, Mum, to make sure I was all right. I felt relieved then and went back to sleep or let go of the dream, whichever it was. Anyway, when I woke up in the morning I felt fine . . .'

As Maurice handed the letter back, the mother said: 'She described you exactly, Maurice, but I hadn't even had time to get in touch with her to tell her I'd asked for help from you!'

My own experience bears out Maurice's story. Only recently a woman rang me from America. She had been suffering from cystitis for some time and asked if I could help.

It was the early hours of the morning and I felt half asleep so I said the only thing I could suggest was that *she* should do the healing and I would ask for help. The next day she rang to tell me what had happened. She went to bed and put her hands over the affected area and felt them getting hot. It was as if they were working independently of her body. Soon she dropped off to sleep while the heat was still coming through. When she woke up she found she had had a lovely rest and the discomfort had gone.

The laws that govern the flow of energy operate at all times. Spirit works on the physical body to encourage it to realign itself with the perfect etheric blueprint. This may happen quickly or take some time according to a range of factors. These will include the condition itself and whether the patient is preventing or encouraging the healing. The most common barriers to healing occur when the patient isn't willing to meet the healer halfway, when they refuse to relax, or when they are frightened. It is not unusual for a patient to refuse to get well and of course it is impossible to work on them if this is the case. A healer cannot make such a person well, and neither can a doctor. A doctor can try all the right medicines but the patient will remain ill. A surgeon can remove all the diseased tissue and still the patient becomes ill again. In such cases the patient is not allowing the God force within to work.

On the other hand, if the patient relaxes and accepts any form of healing or caring they can enjoy the feeling of the God force within them welling up and responding to the energy that is directed towards them. Those who allow themselves to be touched in this way will never be the same again. The force of love will work on them to heal and change their lives for the better, whatever this may mean for that individual. We can rest assured that our own God force knows what it needs to come forth and express itself and for some the changes may be rapid, while for others they are gentle and gradual.

The case studies I have already mentioned show the range of problems that I have had to deal with. In each case a large element of the healing has consisted of listening, allowing the patient to express themselves or get something off their chest. This is part of helping them to relax and enabling me to tune in, and sometimes this is all the patient needs. The spirits can just as easily bring healing into a personal situation as into a physical, mental or emotional problem. This is what I am asked to do when I am approached to give counselling.

The spirits' way is to provide reassurance and a sympathetic ear while they direct love energy towards those involved. While talking, the patient may gradually see a way of solving the problem. If not I give them the support and encouragement to do so. The spirits don't want to make our decisions for us, but they will help and guide us to take responsibility for ourselves and our lives.

Realizing that we (rather than a doctor or some other expert) are responsible for our own health, is part of growing. And realizing how much our bodies have to tell us about this is an essential first step. Healing is not about curing aches and pains, it is about putting people in touch with their real selves. The cure, whatever that might be, is the by-product of this process.

I find that when my patients start talking about themselves and their condition, a pattern of action and reaction is revealed which is the same in very many cases. This pattern is stress and it gives rise to a range of diseases and complaints, many of which are crippling or fatal or both. It is usually generated by pent-up emotions. The cause of this may be outside the patient and concern their reactions to the behaviour of others, no matter how close or distant they might be. Inner causes are more easily identified as negative attitudes either towards themselves or towards others. Whatever the cause, the patient becomes immersed in feelings of resentment, bitterness, fear and hatred. Such feelings give the mind destructive power which soon takes control and before long they find themselves trying to cope with intolerable situations, suppressing their emotions and unable to channel anger and frustration constructively.

Our body reflects this by getting into a state of stress. It is a condition it recognizes as an emergency situation and it stimulates the adrenalin gland to secrete adrenalin. This provides the extra boost to prepare the body for fight or flight and, once secreted, it stays in the body until it is used up by physical exercise. Very few stressful situations we encounter allow us to do this, but the unused hormone will still have its effect. While it encourages increased heartbeat and respiration rates, other functions such as digestion and the continual replacement of body cells are suspended. Soon there is a knock-on effect which begins to spread throughout the body. It wants to return to a state of harmony as quickly as possible so it eventually rebels against the control imposed by the adrenalin. Cell-building, for example, must go on somewhere so a part of the body is found where the control is weakest and soon a growth or so-called 'malignant tissue' is formed.

Stress initiates the secretion of other biochemicals which the body may or may not use up. It must deal with these chemical by-products and if it cannot excrete the excess fast enough, it will store them. Arthritis is a typical example of a chemical deposit which, when accumulated in large enough amounts, brings disease.

The disease, whether physical or mental, tells us something is wrong, but this effect may not manifest itself until some time after the cause. The treatment of symptoms alone only solves the patient's immediate problem. The patient's long-term problem must be attended to if the condition is not to return. So spirit healing encourages the patient to recognize the underlying problem, to identify causes and to find practical solutions. But the healer's function is to heal whatever is damaged whenever this is possible. As well as restoring an injured body or an injured mind, the patient may need a belief in themselves, a love of life, a sense of purpose, a meaningful relationship, a need to love and be loved.

With the pressures in today's waiting rooms and hospitals, doctors and specialists don't have the time to give the patients the sympathetic ear and counselling they might need. Spirit healing treats the patient not the condition. The treatment can therefore vary from patient to patient even though they may be manifesting the same condition.

As I have explained, it is the cause of the condition as much as the condition itself which needs treatment. In most cases, great insight is necessary to discover it, but spirit healing can provide this insight and avoid the need for lengthy and expensive tests and treatment. Unlike the medical profession, we are not always dealing with things as they appear on the surface.

This is why patients so often have to act as guinea pigs while different treatments are tried out on them. Arthritis, for example, has a multitude of causes, ranging from nervous and emotional disorders, a blow on the joint or hormonal imbalance, to circulatory problems. Because of the diagnostic difficulties, many of the treatments involving pharmaceuticals are unnecessary and they produce adverse side effects which cause further problems. If a doctor could tap the resources of a spirit healer to get beyond the symptoms to the cause of the condition, it would bring great savings in time, money and resources which are at present in such short supply.

Working on a patient in 1988, I asked her what treatment she was receiving for her condition. She said her doctor had prescribed antibiotics for a suspected infection. I felt there was a problem with her kidneys and wrote a note to that effect for her to give to the doctor. She went back to see him and he asked her how she was feeling.

'I'm feeling a lot better since I've been to see a spirit healer. He gave me a note for you.'

This doctor was sceptical, but not antagonistic to spirit healing, and wanted to do his best for the patient. So he read my note.

'I wouldn't have thought there was anything wrong with your kidneys, but I'll check them.'

He asked for a urine specimen.

The next day he didn't wait for her to call back, but telephoned her at home. 'The healer was right. There *is* trouble with your kidneys, but we can correct it easily. Don't take any more of the medication I gave you.'

By taking this enlightened attitude, this doctor has allowed us to work together to help many patients whom he has sent to see me. It would be unethical for me to mention all the doctors and specialists who are doing this, but it does show that we are at last drawing closer together. They are realizing that there is a limit to how far we can interfere with the human body. Spirit healing, by going straight to the cause of the patient's problem, minimizes the amount of interference.

A woman came to me in July 1988 with a lump on her ribcage. During the first treatment it got smaller and smaller until it disappeared. The whole treatment, including talking to her and counselling her, lasted just over an hour. She went to hospital simply to get the doctors to confirm that it had gone. If she had had the operation to remove the lump, it would have left a scar, besides interfering with the muscles and nerves in the area. Her body would also have had to cope with any medication, including the anaesthetic, which would have been administered during the hospitalization.

For those patients for whom surgery is necessary, we ask Spirit for help for the patient and also for the surgeon and the medical team. This is how I worked in the case of a woman whose husband was diagnosed as having a wasting disease associated with a problem in the digestive system. In spite of the fact that she didn't believe in spirit healing, she let me know that he was going into hospital for an exploratory operation and that it was a fifty-fifty chance whether they would succeed in finding the trouble. If they could not it was just a matter of time before he would die. I asked her what time the operation would be and said I would do my best, but she was still sceptical.

They prepared him for a major abdominal operation to explore the whole digestive tract. But when the surgeon came to make the first incision, he changed his mind and made a small cut somewhere else. Two stitches were required to close it up again and it was all over.

He came round to see his patient the next day. 'You'll be glad to know we found the cause of the trouble. But I must say it wasn't where I expected it to be. It was just an off chance that I opened you up there and found the problem.'

Something had made him cut in the right place, revealing the obstruction immediately. Yet it had not shown up on the x-ray.

Most healers would like to work more closely with the medical profession for the benefit of the patient. In order to facilitate this, the various healing organizations have got together to form the Confederation of Healing Organizations (CHO) which is compiling a register of approved healers. To be registered, healers must first serve as probationary members of their organization and eventually produce a proven record of their ability and fitness to practise. I look forward to the day when every hospital will be able to call on several appointed healers. Patients would then be able to consult a healer as well as seeing their specialist.

The scope for healing never ceases to amaze me. I wonder how many marriage guidance counsellors would consider themselves to be healers? In the course of my work I have dealt with many couples seeking help and advice on a range of marital issues. I ask the spirits to use me in the usual way and I am sometimes surprised at what I have to say to these people, and the way I have to say it, even to the point of rudeness. This is my spirit helpers' way of making people take a good look at themselves, which they are often reluctant to do. All I know is that it has never been the wrong approach if this was how I was impressed to tackle it. There have even been occasions when, in order to avoid being punched on the nose, I have had to make a hasty exit!

Spirit will take what might seem to be extreme measures when a situation cannot be resolved. I am reminded of a case which appeared intractable until Spirit came through and revealed the husband's infidelity, much to the surprise of the wife and the healer and the astonishment of the husband. He continued to deny his mistress, but Spirit took up the challenge and the more he denied her, the more proof was given. Finally he admitted the truth and Spirit was able to present him with the real issue – whether to acknowledge the wife who loved him and set about rebuilding the marriage or to opt for the mistress

who was causing him a lot of trouble. Spirit would guide
him to make a decision but, as in all cases, the ultimate
choice would be his.

I remember travelling with a couple in a car. We had
quite a complicated journey to make and the wife was
beginning to irritate her husband with her navigational
ideas and suggestions. He began to feel uncomfortable
and his driving deteriorated as the bickering increased.

'Here we go again,' I thought, but instead of allowing
myself to feel embarrassed or ill at ease, I sat back in my
seat and kept quiet and relaxed. Gradually the man began
to relax too and enjoy the drive and so did his wife.

When we got out she said: 'I don't know what you did
to him, Dennis, but he's never been like that before, so
calm and collected. We haven't had such an easy journey
for ages.'

All I had done was relax. In technical terms, I maintained a certain energy field around me which had a positive and soothing effect. This field extended out to influence the others nearby and allowed them to calm down
and relax too, thus defusing the situation.

When Tom surrounded his boss with the colour pink,
he was applying this same natural law and using the
energy of love in a positive manner to change his and
everyone else's life in the workshop for the better (as
described in Chapter Four). The implications of these
simple examples are immense. They demonstrate that it is
within our power to defuse a negative situation any time
we come across it, whether in a personal or social context.
When we see something distressing on the television or in
the newspapers, we don't have to sit there feeling upset
because we can do nothing about it. These conditions
begin with ourselves and occur outside ourselves because
of our own actions and the thoughts we are projecting. So
we can send out a positive constructive thought to the person, animal or place which needs help. No thought or
prayer is ever lost. They are energy forms which sooner or
later must have an effect.

Though I am drawn to working with Spirit in the way I
do, I am aware that, apart from modern orthodox medi-

cine, there are many and varied ways of healing. My helpers in Spirit have all practised different forms of healing, during their various lifetimes, in what would be termed holistic medicine. Many healers today are using similar therapies. I am thinking of practitioners such as herbalists, naturopaths, homeopaths, reflexologists, acupuncturists, and so on, many of whom are applying the energies of Spirit which are contained within the form they are utilizing.

Those who are working to improve our world in some way other than health can also call on the resources of their own spirituality. Spirituality is not a weak, emotional term. It implies the will and ability to create harmony wherever there is disharmony; balance wherever there is imbalance.

We cannot assume that we as individuals are healthy if those in our environment are suffering and this includes the animals, plants and the very earth itself, as well as the human beings. We have been made aware of our planet as a global village and we are becoming aware that it is more importantly a being in its own right. The love force used in healing cannot be confined within the area of health care, but must extend out into all fields of human endeavour.

Understanding who we really are and how we use the different energy systems within, around and beyond us, not only allows us to take control of and responsibility for our own lives, but to enhance the lives of others and safeguard the planet on which we all live. This is healing.

EIGHT
Passing Over

When US astronaut Rusty Schweickart looked down upon the planet earth while working outside his space capsule, he felt the presence of a universal spirit. His experience of this presence so impressed him that he has spent a good deal of time since his NASA mission giving talks about how his life has been changed by it. During a television interview* in Britain he said: 'We are all pressed with our backs against the bomb and our eyes upon the stars.'

I felt this sentiment summed up the mixture of fear and hope which is often in our minds today. The fear is the fear of death by holocaust. The hope is that maybe there is 'someone' out there who can save us from ourselves.

In my early days as a healer it didn't occur to me that healing would encompass so much more than patients and their case studies. I know now that an important element in my work is to dispel fear and to encourage hope. So many people fear the future and the inevitability of their own death. They are fearful and angry, too, that their lives may be cut short by the effects of a nuclear catastrophe or by the violent revolt of the earth itself against the treatment it receives from humankind.

When the subject of death comes up I like to tackle it head-on. I reassure people that Spirit has a purpose on this earth plane and that it cannot be allowed to be destroyed. This is the only intrusion that will be made without invitation. The planet was created for the progression

---

* *Revelations*, ITV, July 1988

of mineral, plant and animal life as well as human experience. It is destined to be a place of trial, tribulation, achievement, enjoyment and happiness for many generations to come.

Naturally, any living system – and this includes our planet – will revolt against maltreatment because it is the law that it must regain its state of balance if this is upset. A good example of this law is our own physical body which constantly seeks to restore us to a state of balance. Our bodies and their sustenance are drawn from the material of the planet so we need to be grateful for this. It also puts upon us the responsibility of joint caretakers. If we duck this responsibility we must not be surprised if we share in the consequences.

We like to think that modern times are full of the greatest uncertainties, yet history shows that life on the earth has always been an uncertain thing. There has only ever been one certainty – that is death. And death is what we most fear.

Fear is dispelled by understanding and I find that fear of death is largely due to a lack of knowledge about what actually happens. Death is the giving up of the physical body when it has served its purpose for this lifetime so that we can pass over into the world of Spirit where we came from. Our life then continues in the world of Spirit. Quite simply, there is no death. Yet the evidence of our eyes would seem to suggest that the giving up of the physical body is pretty final. This is where our fears start and it is why a knowledge of our true selves is so important.

We came here within an etheric body enclosed by a physical one in order to be compatible with the environment of the earth plane. This was to enable us to meet the challenges of this level of existence. But a characteristic of the physical level is that here everything wears out as it gets older and of course this applies to our physical body as well. We take it on for the purposes of experience and, if we look after it properly, it will last for as long as we need it. If the body is abused, it wears out more quickly than it might have done. The time comes when it has either served its purpose or worn out and it is at this moment that we discard it. We die. We move away from the body we have discarded and can see it then devoid of life, for we have taken the *life* with us. Our life carries on in the spiritual and mental dimension which we have also been inhabiting during our time here.

Because we appear to have gone for good, to those on the physical plane it is a day of sadness, but to those on the etheric, our natural habitat, it is a day of rejoicing. We have returned home.

As a medium, I have given proof of this process to thousands when their loved ones in Spirit have come through to talk to them again. Spirit chooses to come through a medium or channeller simply because their psychic senses are developed enough to pick up an etheric presence. But we all have these abilities to a greater or lesser degree, especially where our loved ones are concerned. It is estimated by researchers that at least forty per cent of those who have lost people close to them have experienced their presence shortly after death. This may range from a vague sensation that Spirit is around, to actually seeing, feeling or hearing them. Sometimes spirit visitors move things around or make them fall in order to draw attention to the fact that they are there.

It is quite natural for them to do this for they are concerned about those they have left behind here. They will return again and again to give support and help whenever they can. All they need is an acknowledgement that they are there. I do this by thanking them for coming and I may even ask them if there is anything I can do for them. It is easy to imagine their frustration in being able to see us, knowing that we cannot see them. Acknowledgement strengthens the link and enables them to come closer. In time they may be able to give more and more proof that it is indeed someone we know.

I used to wonder if I would be lucky enough to have the same experience with my own father. Dad wasn't what I would call a religious man, but he respected other people's beliefs. On the occasions he chose to go to a Spiritualist service with me he always came back pretty impressed and we would have a discussion about some point or other until he felt he had grasped it. My mother died when he was in his sixties, and he then went out with a number of women for the next twenty years. He always said he needed more than one partner in case one of them fell ill! After my mother's death, however, his first love was gardening and he continued to work as a gardener for five mornings every week. He only showed signs of slowing down when he had to go into hospital for an operation on his arteries.

I came home from a short trip one day to find a note saying that Dad wasn't very well and could I go and see him? I found him sitting with my brother Ronald, cursing the chiropodist who had been to trim his toenails. He had cut one big toenail too close to the quick and gangrene had set in. I could tell by the way he held his foot that it was very painful. I asked him if I should give him healing. He said 'All right' grudgingly, as if to say 'I'd better humour the idiot', and took his shoe off.

I could smell the gangrene and told him to keep his sock on. I knelt down and put my hands over the foot. In a few moments Chang came through and introduced himself. He called Dad 'the honourable gentleman'. So there I was, on my knees in front of Dad, speaking to him like a high-born mandarin.

Dad took a good look at me. 'You're talking ever so funny, our Den. Are you all right?'

Ronald laughed. 'That's not Den you're talking to, it's his Chinaman!'

Dad seemed none the wiser, but as Chang began talking to him directly he decided to try him out and asked him questions. It wasn't long before he could see that Chang was an alert, intelligent being like himself and a very good conversationalist as well. And so their friendship began.

I got into the habit of seeing Dad every day after that for an hour or two. He would ask if we could have a 'session' so that Chang could come through and talk to him. So for the next few months they discussed everything that interested Dad – history, philosophy, politics, spiritual matters.

Spring came and I booked a holiday on the Broads. Dad said he would miss me and especially his new friend. I told him that Chang would be there with him and not to worry. But two weeks later, when I opened the door to my flat, there was a note saying Dad was in hospital again and to come as quickly as possible.

I was shocked to see how far he had deteriorated. Where I had managed to confine the gangrene to one toe while I had been working on him, now it had spread across to all his toes. The specialist wanted to amputate his leg. I asked Dad if there was anything I could do.

'Yes, there is, Den. I want to talk to Chang.'

So I went and showed the sister my Healing Guild card and said my father wanted some help. She pulled the curtains round us and said we wouldn't be disturbed. I found out later that the specialist had arrived in the middle of our 'session' and the sister asked him to wait while Mr Barrett had healing from his son.

Chang had told Dad about what would happen when he died. Now Dad wanted confirmation of this.

'I have to tell the honourable gentleman that everything I have said on the subject is true. Furthermore, you will die with all your members intact.'

'What about the gardening? Will I be able to carry on with that?'

'Yes, and you will be working in the gardens in the summertime.'

Dad nodded and thought about his next question. 'You said you would be there when the time comes. And my loved ones will come to meet me too?'

'Oh, yes. I can assure the honourable gentleman that we will all be there when you pass over.'

Dad closed his eyes and smiled. He squeezed my hand tightly. 'Thanks, our Den. Everything's all right now.'

Not long after that conversation he woke at six one morning. His pal in the next bed was awake and Dad waved to him. His pal smiled back. The nurse passed by at six-fifteen, went over and saw that he was dead. It was the day they were going to amputate his leg.

A friend of mine recommended a medium who would

give him a Spiritualist funeral as he had requested. I called round to her house as she was about to put her children to bed so we only had a few minutes to talk together. She turned up at the cemetery with a sheaf of notes which her spirit friends had dictated to her about Dad. She read out the notes, which even mentioned his love of flowers and gardening. She had never heard of him before, yet she seemed to know more about him than we did. The service went very well and I was glad that, although many of my relatives were not Spiritualists, they felt comfortable and relaxed.

That Sunday I went to a Spiritualist church and Dad came through to the medium. He told her to tell me that everything Chang had said was right. All the spirit helpers he had made friends with while he was having treatment, and many of the people he had long forgotten from his youth, were there to greet him.

'Tell him it's great!' said Dad. 'And the gardens here are fantastic. If I'd known it was going to be like this, I'd have come over sooner!'

The congregation chuckled and I thought to myself: 'Well, if it's good enough for you, Dad, it's good enough for me, so I'm not at all worried about passing over.'

Now I knew that all the things I had been telling patients about passing over were true because my father had been able to come back and tell me what it was like. He has since decided to work through me and he is often the one giving a patient advice which is direct and to the point, just like he was on the earth plane.

Part of my work is helping people to pass over. If anyone rings me up to say they want some help with a patient who is critically or terminally ill, I try to help them understand my function. We cannot hope to cure everybody and we cannot work against the patient's wish to pass over. My first duty is to the patient and if they are suffering I am not going to do anything to prolong it unnecessarily. I will not keep anyone alive for the sake of the relatives. I can produce enough energy to hold people as they are, but there would be no point in doing it. Nearly all

141

their loved ones can do the same. Anyone can hang on to a patient and delay their passing, but they are doing them a disservice.

Because people are ignorant about their true identity, many do not want to pass when their time is up. The human mind is so strong that it can do almost anything. It can suspend respiration and heartbeat and it can also continue these processes when by normal standards they should have stopped. Somebody may be so afraid, or so reluctant to let go, that they refuse to die. They refuse to relax and go to sleep and they go on suffering as a result.

When I am called to someone in this situation I talk to them about the advantages of dying, and the advantages of being in the spirit world. I tell them that in the last stages of physical life they become linked up with people in Spirit whom they can recognize. It may seem like a dream to the patient, but as they make themselves known, friends and loved ones are recognized who have come to prepare them and help them pass over. Nurses are used to hearing terminal patients talking to them as this stage is reached. The only symptom that is experienced is a gentle drift into a sleep from which they awake in the etheric dimension in their etheric body. The physical carcass is left on the bed. Once the spirit has left the body, animation ceases.

Clairvoyants who have watched people passing over have seen the help being given to raise the spirit in its etheric body from the physical before the heart has stopped beating. True death is the severing of the silver cord, the last link with the physical body. Once this has occurred the body cannot be brought back to physical life. Healers have seen how some patients being kept 'alive' by a life-support machine have already left their body. This is why it cannot be kept alive without the use of a machine.

Even knowing all this, the patient may still wish to prolong their own suffering for their own reasons. I had been visiting Joan for a year. She had so much pain and so many treatments for cancer in the throat, upper chest and face, I didn't know how she could carry on. She had even had operations on her tongue. In her case the cancer was very much a stress-related illness and I had been trying in vain to help her let go of her tensions and problems. She couldn't acccept that she had cancer, that she was very ill and that nothing could be done because of her own attitudes. Time and again she would ask: 'Why me? What have I done to deserve this? I can't understand why this has happened to me. What's it all about?'

I could understand her resentment. She was a woman in her thirites with two young children and a broken marriage. But whatever I said, I knew she was refusing to hear, just as she was resisting all her treatments. Very often counselling plays an important part in helping people with cancer, but in her case it didn't seem to work.

One day I had a call from her doctor at the hospice asking if I would visit her again. When I arrived he wanted to see me first to discuss his patient. We talked at length about the hopelessness of the situation from his side. I told him about my viewpoint and the possibilities that Spirit has to help people. The spirits intimated, through me, that the young woman was at a crossroads and she either had to sink or swim. They would prefer it if she swam, but they didn't think there was much chance of that so they would do their best to make sure that she did not suffer unnecessarily.

The doctor heaved a sigh of relief. 'Well, Mr Barrett, if you can do that you'll be working a miracle because none of our treatments have been effective and we don't know why. Sleeping tablets don't work with her and neither do the painkillers. Please go and see what you can do for her.'

I went and sat with her for a couple of hours and this time we seemed to get on very well. She had a job to speak because of her condition, but she did manage to let me know what she was feeling. I did my best to reassure her that she was in good hands. The future would be a lot brighter for her if she would give people the chance to help her. I had to go then because her other visitors were due.

In the early evening, the duty sister telephoned to ask me if I would see Joan again. I went in and stayed with her until about midnight. We talked about life after death and the opportunities she would have in Spirit to help her loved ones which she didn't have in her present state of illness.

Finally she loosened up and revealed one of the reasons why she found it so difficult to let go and relax. She had always been afraid of being pronounced dead while she was still alive. When she was a child she had been told a horror story along these lines and the image had lodged in her mind for the rest of her life. This was the barrier she had put up to relaxing and accepting her sleeping tablets and going to sleep. I promised her I wouldn't leave her while she was asleep so that if she woke up I would still be with her. I also promised her that in the event of her passing I would check with the doctors that she had every test before they pronounced her passed over.

The night nurse came on at ten to give out the medication to all the patients and I left the ward while they were looking after Joan. The night nurse came out and said: 'There's no need for you to stay, Mr Barrett.'

'I think I should stay. This lady is afraid of going to sleep and waking up to find that she hasn't passed over, but has still been pronounced dead.'

'That's ridiculous. We don't do things like that. But I'm glad you told me. I didn't realize she was so frightened of such a thing happening. If you want to go home, I'll stay with her and do my knitting in here so she'll have somebody with her all the time she's asleep.'

They had made Joan comfortable and drawn back the curtains. I went over and told her that the night nurse was going to relieve me and would be staying with her all through the night. She nodded and soon she dropped off to sleep holding my hand. The nurse arrived at midnight with her knitting and promised she wouldn't let me down. It was a Friday night. I asked her to give me a ring when Joan woke up again and set off for home. I had done my best and I handed the case over to Spirit.

I never received a call until Sunday afternoon. Joan's mother had gone in and sat with her while she was still sleeping and she passed peacefully without waking up again. I have heard from Joan since, through mediums. She is fit again and says she finds she can do more for her children now than she could before her illness. She is with them constantly and she knows that they are well aware of her presence. She thanked me for keeping my promise and I was thankful that once again the spirits had kept theirs.

During my talks with her doctor, Spirit intimated that it was not the condition that was hopeless, but Joan herself and I find that my medical friends have come across the same phenomenon. There is no hopeless condition, but there are hopeless people. The difference is vast. There is no illness I know of which is incurable, not even AIDS. In all cases the human body wants to be well and it wants the opportunity to heal itself. Provided there is a chance for it to recover, it can reverse conditions which appear to be hopeless. It has been proved to me over and over again that it is the patient who is incurable and not the illness.

We do not realize how strong the power of the mind is. Patients may be incurable simply because they are using this power against themselves and they will not change their way of thinking. Others will not change their way of living. Still others cannot prevent the build-up of stress within themselves and this eventually takes its toll. If we can help people to relax they can get over complaints they thought were terminal. We have to help ourselves by allowing the God force within to prevail and put the body right. Spirit doesn't want to cart a carcass around which is damaged by illness or disease, but if the physical body is overcome and baffled by stress, wrong thinking or thoughtless living, the spirit cannot prevail. It is forced to depart from the physical body and go back to the spiritual dimension.

Sometimes people see the light and realize that their body is indeed trying to tell them something. Acknowledging this is the first step back to health. The second one is to tune in to our selves and patiently listen to what the body is saying to us. Once we know this, it is our responsibility to act and to change things.

I was treating a patient recently for cancer of the breast. Elizabeth had come to me because the specialist had told her that the condition was so far gone there was no point in removing her breast because there was no hope of saving her life anyway.

One day she said to me: 'Do you know, Dennis, the best news I've ever had was when they told me I had cancer.'

I must have looked surprised for she became quite adamant about it. 'Yes, I really mean it. It was the best news I had ever had.'

'Why do you say that, then?'

'It pulled me up short. I had to stop and take a good look at myself and where I was going wrong. I spent my life planning for the future, worrying about tomorrow. Now I live for today and I enjoy it. I've stopped striving.'

She had put so much effort into preparing for the eventualities she expected that she was unprepared for those which finally overtook her. Her body rebelled against the stress and strain she was imposing on herself and she became ill. She was a successful businesswoman with a wonderful sense of humour, yet if someone cracked a joke in the office she would bite their heads off and order them to get back to their work.

'I was horrible to live with. But when my body began to go wrong, I realized I was being unkind to myself. Something had to change and I've changed it!'

She began to recover and was soon back to being a normal healthy woman. Eventually there wasn't even a trace of a lump in her breast. She had recovered from what had been diagnosed as an incurable disease. On her last visit to me she admitted she had been a difficult person, but now everybody found it enjoyable to be with her. 'You know, Dennis, I must have been a real pain before!'

Elizabeth realized that her healing wasn't so much about making her body better, it was her mind that needed help. Once Spirit had helped her to work on her mind, her body was able to realign itself with its etheric blueprint. She had listened to her body and taken the advice of her own God force to use her mind in a positive and constructive way.

The purpose of healing is to help people live and life goes on forever, whether it is in the physical body or not. I am not trying to extend anyone's earthly life or even to cure their aches and pains, I am trying to heal them so that they can take up the way of life their spirit wants them to take. Healing may therefore involve helping them to come to terms with themselves or those around them or perhaps even their own death.

There are many reasons why people cannot come to terms with their own death after they have passed over. The most common of these is that they know nothing about it. Among this group are those who die suddenly as a result of an explosion, accident or disaster of some kind. Other members of this group could be people who either did not believe in the continuation of life or could not possibly conceive of it. Many such spirits find themselves wandering around on the earth plane among places that are familiar to them, yet no one seems to recognize them any more or take any notice of them. They need help from those in Spirit, or a medium who can communicate with them, to explain what has happened so that they can be gently guided into the spirit world.

Sometimes the passing of a spirit is so traumatic that they are unable to let go of the circumstances, the pain or suffering involved. This accounts for what are known as 'ghosts', people who cannot leave the scene of their death or may want to warn others about it and appear to be trapped in time, as it were. Again, they need help to come to terms with the fact that they are now in Spirit and can get on with their lives.

Finally, there are spirits who were quite content with their earthly life and intend to carry on with it, being ignorant of the fact that they have passed over. (Examples of both the above cases are described in Chapter Four.)

People ask me how we can tell when our time is up. If they knew when this was to be, they say, they would make better use of their lives. Others don't want to know because they wouldn't like to live in fear of that moment. The fact that we don't know the time of our death means we should enjoy life, taking it day by day and living it to the full. If there is something put before us to do it is best to do it wholeheartedly since we don't know how much time we have in which to complete it. For the same reason, if the chance comes to apologize, make amends or resolve a difference, we shouldn't hesitate until it is too late.

We come here for a purpose which is unique to us and when we have achieved it we have no more need to be here. Sometimes we lose sight of that purpose, but we are subject to natural law and if our body has had enough we have to depart without having achieved our aim. So we cannot judge each other. Sometimes Spirit simply needs the experience of being a baby and so it dies in infancy. Sometimes it has come to help its parents and once the task is complete it dies in childhood. Spirit is a part of the God force, it is neither baby, nor child nor adult, but an evolving spirit entity at a certain level of progression.

Others appear to die due to various circumstances, but it becomes obvious that it is not time for them to pass over; they still have something left to do here. In 1984 I was out shopping in Bristol. One moment I was looking in a shop window and the next thing I knew I was waking up in hospital. They said I had collapsed with heart trouble. I didn't feel too concerned at the time because they had made me quite comfortable. I was told to rest for a few hours and then I was allowed home.

However, this was the shape of things to come and in the middle of 1985 the same thing happened again. This time I woke up in hospital to find a number of medical personnel standing over me and various tubes and wires attached to my body.

'Hello there, are you Dennis Barrett?'

'Yes, I am.'

'You've had a lucky escape, Mr Barrett. We're having a problem trying to understand what happened to you, so we'd like to keep you in intensive care for a few days. All right?'

I had gone out in the morning and come round in the evening so I had been unconscious for most of the day. After two days I was moved into an ordinary ward and the

148

following day the specialist came to see me. 'We can't find anything wrong with you now, Mr Barrett.'

'Can I go home then?'

'If you feel up to it, whenever you like.'

A month later I had an appointment to see the same doctor. She couldn't find anything wrong with me, but she wanted to check that things were still all right. I asked her what had happened to me.

'You had all the symptoms at the time of a massive heart attack. Your heart was fibrillating.'

'What was that?'

'Your heart was fluttering so much there was no blood circulation. In other words your brain was starved of oxygen and it had stopped functioning. Your respiration also stopped, but we managed to stabilize your heart. Technically speaking, Mr Barrett, you were dead for a time.'

I sat there stunned. I had no memory whatsoever of an out-of-body experience. I could recall nothing.

'But I'm all right now?' I asked her.

'That's what we find difficult to understand. There are no signs now that you ever had the attack. You seem to be a perfectly healthy man for your weight.'

'My weight?'

'It would help if you lost some weight. Too much body weight puts an extra strain on the heart as you probably know.'

As I went home with my clean bill of health I thought about my 'death'. I was sorry that I knew so little about it and could only conclude that my time had not yet come. Perhaps there was more work for me to do. But was there anything left for me that someone else couldn't do just as well?

A few days later I went to a public demonstration of clairvoyance in the big hall on College Green in Bristol. The medium was Gordon Higginson who is the principal of the Arthur Findlay College, Stansted Hall. Many consider him to be one of the best mediums in the world, myself included. There were about six hundred people in the audience when Gordon walked out onto the platform. After introducing himself he came to me first. I had a seat towards the back of the hall and he pointed in my general direction.

'I am sure there is somebody in that area there who would recognize a very unusual name, F–. It is the name of a German gentleman. I feel he used to serve your church and I feel he has only recently passed over.'

Nobody else claimed this person so I said that I could recognize him.

'I can give you the first name of this man's wife which is Freda. You ought to recognize that name too.'

'Yes, I do,' I said.

'Good. Well I want to move away from you, down to the front here. I have to link up with a lady called Audrey.' He pointed to a woman who was sitting at the front. She was a personal friend of mine and of the man and woman he had already mentioned. He had made the link and he was spot on, in spite of the fact that there were two or three hundred people between us.

'But I've got to come back to you now,' he continued. 'You've been ill, no, you've been in hospital haven't you?'

'Yes.'

'They didn't know what was wrong with you though, did they?'

'No, that's right.'

He was smiling at me now. 'We know. Spirit is telling me you died. You passed over, your time was up. You were finished!'

I found myself gasping with surprise and managed to croak, 'Oh, ah . . .'

'But Spirit says they heard the prayers going up from all the people who know you and they decided to let you come back and do some more. You're a worker, aren't you?'

He was nodding almost before I could reply. 'They also said you should lose weight. Spirit is saying "That's true, you *ought* to lose weight".'

'Thank you very much!'

But Gordon hadn't finished. 'If you can lose another three stone – '

'I'd rather be over there!'

He laughed, along with the audience. 'If you can, you'll have at least another eight years to set the world on fire if you want to!'

The audience laughed again and I laughed too, but it got me thinking. I had recently been made redundant so I was free. Free to set the world on fire? I decided then and there that every day from then on would be a bonus. Whatever opportunities Spirit put in my way I would meet with a resounding 'Yes!'

My own case interested me particularly because of a modern phenomenon caused by the revival of patients from so-called clinical death. The experience of many such patients of being separated from their physical body, yet retaining full consciousness, is now well documented by such researchers as Dr Elisabeth Kübler-Ross and the Michaelmas Trust. The patients testify to an awareness of other dimensions of reality beyond the physical, accompanied by overwhelming feelings of peace, harmony and love. They become convinced that consciousness continues after death and that their physical body is not 'them'. This usually leads to a transformation of their attitudes and a reappraisal of their lives, besides taking away the fear of death. Such descriptions are now so universally consistent they have come to be known as the 'Near Death Experience' (or NDE).

Spirit told me that in my own case I was returned to the point where my brain had stopped functioning. This meant that there was no time lapse in which my brain might have ceased operating and therefore no interruption in the brain pattern. Perhaps this was why I had no NDE. Nevertheless, the exciting thing for me about the research evidence is that it backs up the descriptions given by those who have passed over and have come to tell us about it through a medium. Ironically, modern science, which has for so long denied anything that it cannot measure, has provided the means whereby people have gone through the experience of passing over and been able to come back and talk about it in the physical body. Each one of them has brought us a brief personal glimpse

151

of the world of Spirit, the sum total of which lends tremendous support to those in Spirit who are trying to help us in our understanding of their world.

I have based my knowledge of life after death on what I have been told by my spirit guides and helpers, by my own father and of course the many thousands in Spirit who have either come through me or through other mediums. For me the truth of these descriptions is that whereas life on the earth plane is bounded by the dimensions of time and space, life beyond this level is a state of being where time and space are no longer relevant. Instead, other dimensions and other meanings apply. Of course this makes it even more difficult for the spirits to use the language of the earth plane in which to express such concepts.

The first thing that becomes apparent is that we have moved up from the relative denseness of the physical to a level of higher vibration. Here, our senses are extended and are more finely tuned. We see colours and hear sounds, for example, which we could not have imagined before passing over. Yet relativity prevails on all levels. Things appear to be just as solid as they were on the physical level. Our etheric body and the bodies of others are firm to the touch. But now there is a fundamental difference. Here, thought is paramount and the will is supreme. The world of Spirit is whatever we want or indeed think it to be. We can choose our surroundings, live how we like and be any 'age' we like. We can also travel anywhere in an instant. This is why one of my helpers can be working with me in Bristol and with someone in Australia at the same time. The only limitations are those imposed by ourselves because our imaginations will not extend any further.

When we go to sleep we tend to spend a part of this time in astral travelling, travelling on those planes outside the earth. We do this in our etheric body. During this time we can meet up with people here on earth, with those who have passed over and those in our true spirit family. We also meet all kinds of teachers who are there to give us the benefit of their knowledge and wisdom. We have in fact been making regular visits to our true home from the moment of birth. There is a transition time after birth for us to get used to being here, which is one of the reasons why babies need so much sleep – they still need time in the spirit world. So I can assure my patients that when they pass over things will be quite familiar to them.

Perhaps most important of all is the fact that we have moved back closer to the source of love and its influence is much more apparent. Now our own vibrations reveal exactly who we are. Other spirits can tell so much about us by seeing into our aura and by 'feeling' it. It reveals our state of spiritual development. The truth cannot be kept secret here because it is available to those who want to see.

The God force contains a record of every thought, act and experience we have ever had or done in the memory of the subconscious mind. So we are able to look back over the life we have just left and assess it. We see ourselves as we are. We become aware of the law of cause and effect and how whatever future we choose must inevitably make provision for the balancing of the effects we have brought into being by our own thoughts and actions. With the help of those who love us, we can decide whether to incarnate again to gain other earthly experience or whether to continue in the spirit world.

People who have developed to the point where they no longer need the experience of the earth plane are given the opportunity to progress by working through human beings whom they call 'instruments'. They are not restricted to the field of healing of course. It soon becomes apparent that any spirit who is working through us or with us and is able to do things which appear to be 'miraculous' is a personality of a high order. My helpers have told me that their opportunities to progress in this way are limitless since they can avail themselves of the higher spiritual energies and the higher levels of development. The knowledge and resources presented by this opportunity are passed down through the chain of being to the humans who are acting as their instruments and through them to the patients or others for whom they may be working. In this way the link of love is used by Spirit to bring great benefit to humanity.

I am a bit of a sceptic myself and I don't go along with anything I can't accept or which I can't prove to my own satisfaction. I accept everything I have mentioned in this chapter regarding death (or passing over, as I prefer to call it), but in spite of my own clinical death, my experience of it was still academic until the first morning of October 1988. I woke up in the early hours knowing I had just had an important experience. It was one of the few times I have ever remembered a dream so vividly and I felt I had to record it. When I played the recording back to myself I realized I had not been dreaming, but had been given the experience of my own death.

I was sitting in a sports stadium surrounded by people who were watching something that seemed like a football match. A man came and stood beside me. He spoke to me gently: 'I have to tell you that it's nearly time for you to die.'

Strangely, I felt no apprehension and found myself nodding and saying: 'All right, when will it be?'

I looked up at him and saw a well-built man of between fifty and sixty with a kind, smiling face, dressed in what seemed like a very long fawn-coloured raincoat. It was open at the neck and he wore a collar and tie.

'I'll come for you when it is time.'

I thanked him and he left me to my own thoughts which took me immediately back into the past. I thought of the people I had known, especially my family. My daughter came to mind. I knew I had caused her pain when my first marriage broke up. Was there a way I could have avoided it? I thought of my son and his family and felt happy for them all. I thought of the people I had worked with and my reactions to them.

I was musing over the past like this, wondering if I could have done anything differently, whether I could have changed things, when a hand touched mine. It was my friend again.

'It's time,' he said.

'All right.'

I got up and he held my hand as we threaded our way through the rows of seats. Nobody took any notice of us. It was as if there was five feet of space between the rows and we could walk without touching anyone. We walked out of the stadium and on through the streets. Everything seemed normal. But soon the houses changed to buildings like long nissen huts made of some strange material like asbestos. My companion still held my hand as we walked and said nothing.

The thought came to my mind: 'I'm relieved. I've had enough. I don't really want to carry on living. I wonder how it's going to end, what comes next?'

Just then he stopped and walked towards one of the buildings and drank some water from a cup. I held out my hand for some water, but he just smiled and said nothing. He took my hand and we went on. I felt like a child being led by its mother.

'What comes next?' I asked him. But he would not reply.

I tugged at his hand and asked again: 'What comes next?'

His lips moved, but I heard no sound. I felt annoyed. I didn't like being treated like a little child. Then the thought came: 'But you are *acting* like a little child. Start to think.'

I looked back at him and said: 'But what have I got to think?'

He smiled again and said to me mentally: 'Think of anything.'

I asked: 'How am I to die?' But this time I thought it.

'You already have.'

Suddenly, as he 'spoke' these words, I realized he was no stranger. I had known him all my life, during many incarnations.

'How did it happen?'

He nodded and raised the hand that had been holding mine and gestured towards the place we had walked away from. I turned and was back on the terrace, among the rows of people. I was standing in front of my own physical body and saw that my head had fallen forward onto my chest. No one around me had realized that I had died.

He thought to me, and the words came into my mind as clear as if I was listening to someone speaking: 'It is all over. Think again.'

And I thought: 'What will come after this?'

He held his hand up. 'Be at peace.'

Now people were thronging round the dead body which was mine, treating it as if it was someone to be helped rather than be afraid of.

My companion and I left. That part of me which was still present on those terraces held no interest for me any more. I was reborn. He smiled. 'Think.'

'Where do we go from here?'

'Anywhere!'

My thoughts were becoming stronger. I wanted to see it all.

'Wait,' he said. 'Now we will go and see the rest of the family.'

I no longer held his hand. I was looking forward to my new status and I wanted to get on with living. I wanted to fly all over the world and see everything at once. My heart wasn't beating, but there seemed to be that throb of expectancy. There was no feeling of tiredness, yet we seemed to have walked forever. We had travelled far, yet we had been nowhere.

He smiled. 'That's true. We've covered the ground, but we haven't used our own energy to do it. We have used the power of our thoughts, the power of our minds. You can do anything in your mind. Is there anything you would like to do before we go into the family group?'

'Yes. I want to see my children.'

'Right. But they won't see you. Think.'

I thought of my daughter and was immediately in her presence as she sat working at a knitting machine. She was relaxed and enjoying what she was doing. I didn't want to intrude on her and I stood back.

Again he said: 'Think.'

I thought of my son and as quick as a flash I was with him. He was talking to one child while he held the other. He was explaining to the older one how he could help himself by having another go at the puzzle before him. I stood back and watched them being happy together.

'Think.'

I thought of all the things I had left undone on the earth plane and I realized there was no way I was going to be able to change them. Now I no longer wanted to. I was free, free of all the hustle and bustle of everyday life. I was free of all the worry about how to pay my bills, free of the fear of making a mistake. I was suddenly aware that I had always lived in fear of hurting people by my thoughtlessness and now I was free of that fear too. I had shrugged off a burden and was able to appreciate the lightness of my new conditions.

I was aware of my breathing. I had always been short of breath. 'Do I breathe? Will I hurt myself if I hold my breath?' And I realized that my new body didn't survive on oxygen and food. I began to take an interest in myself and what I looked like. As I thought of a mirror, there it was in front of me, a full-length mirror. I looked into it and saw the one I always took to be me – an older person in an everyday suit, tall, of indiscriminate shape, with a darkish complexion and greying hair – looking back at me.

Now I didn't hesitate. I thought of myself when I was a child. And there I was, a child of eight with knee-length trousers, jersey and tousled hair. Then I was a young man at the end of the war, tackling the world head-on, full of my own self and my own capacity to do anything. I had been sure then that those around me never realized just how strong and capable I was and how upright. Yet now I could be exactly what I wanted.

My friend had moved away from me.

'Why have you left now?' I asked him.

'You no longer need my help or my guidance.'

I looked around without any feeling of panic. I was curious. 'There has to be something more. What comes next?'

With that I was transported into a group of a dozen or so people of varying ages, all perfectly normal in every way. There was nothing wraithlike about anyone, but I knew of course that I was now in the world of Spirit. This was home, not a different dimension, and the people I was with were people I knew. There was Marge, Ethel and Grace. There was Charlie, and Tom, and there . . . was Chang! The one who had helped me when I was on the earth plane and worked through me, and talked to my dad, and talked to so many others, was standing looking at me.

I watched and waited. If I had been breathing I would have said 'with bated breath'. Chang walked towards me and I knew I had known him during all my lifetimes, for all of time. He greeted me with open arms. We embraced and looked into each other's eyes. Without saying, we knew that we were going to continue to live a life which included each other and which included all our friends. The men and women whom I had been close to all my life were there and we were going to continue being together.

I felt satisfied. I didn't want to know any more. It was enough that I had come home. As these thoughts went through my mind I never heard a sound, I *felt* sound. I sensed beautiful impressions that seemed stronger than anything I had felt during my past life on earth. This was the place I had always known and earth was a thing of the distant past.

I didn't need to ask 'What comes next?' because I knew now, I had done it so many times before. I had come back home so often and each time I had returned, the routine was a different one. Without asking any more questions, I knew that I could do what I liked. I could sit and learn from other people who would come and touch me on a mental wavelength, as my friend had come to touch me and take me from my physical body. They would fill me with thoughts and knowledge, guidance and wisdom.

I was more than happy, I was content. Above all, I was ready, ready to continue my journey, ready to explore the many ways in which I could be of service to those I had left behind, freed from the limitations of my physical body.

As I switched off the recorder I found myself musing on the whole experience. Even as I listened, part of me was still 'there' where it had all taken place. I needed time to get completely back into my body.

I thought about the stadium and wondered whether that was where I would be when it happened or whether the image was a symbolic one. Since I started treating patients in my own home, I have led what many might call a solitary life, yet I died surrounded by a crowd of people, fans even. Could they have been the thousands who have come my way, whom Spirit and I have tried to help?

It is difficult to explain something we haven't experienced ourselves. But now that I have had a practical demonstration, I feel I have been given the experience to pass on. Some people will feel all the better for reading it. For others it may answer an important question. One thing I am certain of is that it will enhance my efforts in helping people to pass over.

We planned this chapter about passing because much of my work has been with the incurable and the terminally ill. We wanted our readers to understand how death fits into the picture, that it is going home, and truly an important part of the ongoing adventure of living. It is not the end of everything, but the continuation. Whatever illnesses or infirmities we have at the time of passing are left behind with the physical carcass. The only thing we take with us as Spirit is the memory which the God force within needs for our personal experience. For people who are aware of these realities, passing over is a time of peace and joy. This is the message we want to get across.

NINE

Birth and Reincarnation

'We are born because we choose to be born.'

For some of my patients this is the most provocative statement I can make, especially those who are suffering mentally or physically. Though death is the thing we fear most, I find people can accept what I tell them about passing over and life after death more easily than when I talk about birth and their own reasons for being here.

Suffering is difficult to come to terms with, but an understanding of why we are here goes a long way towards helping us to do so. It took me some time to reach this understanding and I am thankful that meanwhile Spirit helped me to cope with my own suffering by giving me the opportunity to look away from myself towards others.

Many of my patients don't realize that life has to make sense to me too and that I am no different to them in this respect. I have lived an ordinary life and faced the problems of growing up, marriage, family and work. Like everyone else, I have encountered plenty of obstacles and many painful situations along the way. And the many mistakes I've made have taught me as much as my achievements and are therefore just as valuable.

But life has also thrown up so many questions which seemed unanswerable at the time. Even though friends, mediums and healers came up with some of the answers, I still sensed the unanswered question: how and where did I fit into the picture? I had to realize that the answers could not be found outside myself; I had to take time to relax and

listen to my inner voice, the voice of my true self. Finally I
came to accept that, if I was the God force within, I was responsible for my being here. Having made this choice, I
could progress by meeting the challenges life put in front
of me. I was responsible for what had happened to me so I
couldn't blame other people.

Reaching this understanding and accepting this responsibility was a kind of liberation. At last I was in charge of
my own destiny. The whole process of painful discovery
had brought me to the realization that each and every one
of us comes here to do something which only we can do.
This is our reason for living. The mystery of life for me is
not how it happens, but why.

As I mentioned in the previous chapter, the decision to
come here is made back in our true home in the world of
Spirit. In consultation with our own spirit family and perhaps other entities also, we evaluate which stage we have
reached on our life journey. From this evaluation we
decide whether to come to the earth plane or whether to
progress on the other planes of existence. Certain experiences can only be had here so this is an important fac-
tor in helping us to make a decision. We may decide to
come for a number of reasons. For example, to learn more
from earth plane experiences, to teach others, to help
others, to be an example to others or to balance out the
effects of past actions. All these reasons are linked to the
particular spirit's stage of development.

Once the decision to come is made, we choose the conditions which will give us the challenges in life which we
require. This means that we choose the sex we wish to be
and the family to be born into, which includes both our
parents and any brothers or sisters. We also choose the
type of environment as well as the period in time to be
born into and we are provided with the physical and
mental attributes we shall need. Contrary to what many of
my patients think, no one comes here with a job to do
which is beyond their capabilities. But just as we choose
our parents, and so on, to give us the challenges we require, so we also bring with us something which will pro-

161

vide challenges for others.

Birth on the earth plane signifies a decisive point on the journey of life. It is so important that we wait for a number of forces to coincide – spiritual, cosmic, solar, earthly – before we are ready to be born. The exact moment is recorded both in our subconscious mind and in the etheric records. Many in the world of Spirit are watching when each and every one of us makes our departure and they continue to watch over us until we return.

Having decided to come to earth, for whatever reason, we are given a broad outline of what we are going to be aiming for once we get here. From the moment of physical birth, though, this knowledge is wiped away from the conscious mind and kept in the subconscious mind so that we start with a clean slate, so to speak. The script of life has not been written out for us word for word. Even so, some of the players seem to need a clearly defined script, while others make it up as they go along. Most of us ad lib a bit and tend to broaden the part as a result. Our part is the person we came to be. We are kept to this part by the prompter, our guide.

Just as I have a healing guide who teaches me about healing and guides me in what I do, we all have a guide or guardian angel who is appointed as our prompter in life. This is a highly evolved being whose function is to watch over us and nudge us when we go off the track, so that we can encounter those things which we came to experience. There have been many occasions when my guide has had to shout his loudest as I was about to take a wrong turning!

When we are born our guide is very close to us and their voice is strong and easy to hear. This is what is known as the 'still small voice' or voice of conscience. If we relax quietly and allow the God force within to speak to us, we hear this same voice.

When patients complain to me of feeling alone, I tell them about their guide who is always with them. The guide's role is not to spare us from experience, however, or to interfere with our free will. People misunderstand this and often feel forsaken, but this is because they have distanced themselves from their guide by their feelings. When someone asks me why the guide doesn't save us from some problem or difficulty, I take them back to their original decision to come here. If we let someone else face our problems or perform our tasks for us then we are denying this decision. We have to do the learning and growing, our guide cannot do it for us; just as a parent cannot walk for their child, it must learn to walk for itself. We put ourselves in a particular situation in order to face the challenges that it presents and it would be a denial of our true self, our self responsibility and our learning experience, if we tried to avoid it.

As we grow up and go out into the world we tend to submerge the voice of conscience for various reasons, many of which are to do with survival. Like other people, I felt the need to conform and sometimes this brought about a conflict with my conscience, so I stifled its voice when I didn't want to hear it. When we do this, our guide is pushed back a little. But free will reigns and we have to remember that Spirit cannot interfere. If necessary we will just have to learn by our own mistakes. Happily, most of us have the chance to appreciate that there is a spiritual dimension to life and the voice of our guide can begin to make itself heard again, to encourage and urge us on to overcome the obstacles on the path.

Their role is also to protect and guard. In the world of Spirit, as well as highly developed souls, such as our guides, there are far less developed souls. People are not reformed by passing over. They are exactly the same as they were on the earth plane and we may need to be protected from them or their influence.

When people delve into things of a 'psychic' nature and concentrate on developing this aspect alone, they leave the door open to such influences from the world of Spirit. If we want to lower our standards in this way our guardian angel is disarmed and cannot stop us. For this reason it is essential to approach all knowledge from a spiritual point of view and try to develop spiritually as well as in every other way. This allows the guide to protect us from negative and lowly developed influences. We only have to ask for what is right and good and the arms of our guide are strengthened when they are standing at the doorway to our mind, our heart and our body. Then they can say: 'Only the best shall come through here.'

More common, of course, are the situations which make us deviate from our purpose. Apart from the obvious ones of killing, stealing or lying, there are all those things that originate from human fears and desires – cruelty, selfishness, thoughtlessness, revenge, betrayal, infidelity, greed, and so on. When any situation occurs which tempts us to give in to such thoughts or actions, our guide tries to get through and help us to say no. In life, decisions and choices have to be made and the guide is always on hand to help us make the best one.

The purpose of our guide is identical with that of our own spirit so that if we listen to the dictates of our conscience we can do nothing wrong and we will always be taking the quickest pathway to our goal in life. This goal may well be to learn a vital lesson which can only be learned in this environment, in this body, in this set of circumstances. Or we may be born for several other reasons. We may come as an object lesson for someone else or as an opportunity for others to benefit from. We don't all come to learn. Some come to teach through the example or circumstances of their life. We choose our life and the obstacles we are going to face, for the purposes of our own development. We do not know when another has achieved their purpose so they may appear to depart at what we would call the wrong time.

Spirit in the form of some children may seem to come here for all the wrong reasons. They might be unwanted, wanted for what their parents can get out of them, or born into terrible circumstances. But in all cases, Spirit's progress, the child's life, is planned, even if it is simply to provide their parents with opportunities to understand themselves and to come to grips with their own frailties, or not, as the case may be.

We each have a unique destiny and it is no one's place to interfere with this. If we can learn to accept the lives of others as they are, we may be able to accept our own life as the natural result of a choice we have made. We can stop wondering why something has been inflicted on us or what we have done to deserve it because life is not something we have been condemned to.

Parents have asked me why a particular illness has struck their child. Why couldn't it have happened to them instead? I explain that we cannot take on someone else's lessons. There is an experience for the child in coping with the illness and quite a different one in their caring for the child. Both experiences are important to the spirits involved.

Over the years I have worked with many disabled people and my approach is firstly not to focus on their disability, but to get them to think about their role in relation to others. This raises their awareness and puts them in the context of Spirit achieving its own special purpose in being here. When I have been confronted with the question of how a disabled person can make the kind of contribution they would like to make to society, I start by trying to get them to see through the physical situation to the spiritual one beneath.

From a spiritual point of view, the state of the body or mind is Spirit's attribute, not lack or disability. It is what Spirit has chosen to carry out its task, therefore it is the most perfect means of doing this. It is Spirit's challenge, not the challenge of those looking on. Their challenge is in how they react, whether they turn their backs or whether they care.

The finest steel has been tempered in the hottest furnace. The more advanced we are, the harder the challenges we are going to choose. The person who never seems to have anything to cope with is at a young stage of progression as a spiritual being. The more advanced spirit who has more to put up with has already met the elementary challenges of life in previous incarnations. Opportunities are chosen as well as disappointments, for the human being seems to progress more by experiencing pain and by overcoming difficulties and in fact thrives on a challenge. I can't question their purpose in life and for this reason I cannot judge anyone.

Secondly, they may have come here in order to teach, rather than to learn. They can teach others how to cope, and how to adapt in spite of extreme difficulty. Other people see the disabled body or the disabled mind. But Spirit is whole and simply functioning through a particular physical body or a particular brain. We must look within to link up with the God force and the source of our own love.

Thirdly, I ask them if they have ever thought that they provide opportunities for the advancement of others, starting with their parents and continuing with every person they encounter in their lives. And these encounters can be with people they never meet. People may hear about them, read about them or see them on television. Every such encounter provides an opportunity for someone else to care, perhaps changing a prejudice or attitude.

All these aspects of such people are a tremendous contribution to life on the earth plane and a contribution which I as a healer cannot make. They heal and they teach in their own way.

One of the things I have learned in healing is not to judge someone by the image they are purposely projecting. I have learned, for example, that some of the people who seem to have little intelligence or mental ability are very often highly developed souls who have come to give people the opportunity to learn through encountering their simplicity. When we go into a hospital and see a person drooling and babbling, perhaps flapping their limbs about, we may turn away and dismiss them. This is a big mistake. Spirit is not disabled or defective, but is at all times an evolving being on its journey of life.

The Hopi Indians are great philosophers and one of their sayings is useful in helping us to come to terms with difficult situations: 'It is not what comes which matters, but how we behave when it does.'

In a given situation we see one person who accepts and makes the best of it while another complains bitterly and may even be overcome by it. We all have to learn to adapt to things that happen to us and this also means that we shouldn't stand in the way of others who have to learn too. Tolerance of our own frailties and those of others goes a long way to aiding the general progress of Spirit.

People learn their lessons at different rates and some may take a lot longer to learn the same lesson than others. Our inner self wants us to have a certain experience, but it may not happen because we are not ready for it. If it does happen and we aren't ready, we may not be able to learn from it. Readiness is crucial to learning and when that moment comes for someone, we may be instrumental in bringing it about.

One evening I was invited to take part in a discussion with a group of people who were interested in my views. Among other things, the subject of birth and reincarnation came up. One of the women present insisted on answering every question that was put to me which effectively prevented her friends from hearing what I had to say. After a few scornful remarks she said: 'Well, I would like to know what I'm here for.'

At this, my spirit helpers rose to the challenge: 'We'll certainly tell you what you came here for, but you won't like what we have to say.'

They described several of her previous lifetimes during which she had held many aristocratic positions. Again she had been wealthy all her life, but she still hadn't learned an important lesson which was to accept other people as they are and to accept their views.

She hardly waited for me to stop talking before she responded angrily. 'What rubbish! I've always taken people as they are. I never try to change people.'

Her daughter turned to her and said: 'But it's all true, Mum. We could have told you, but we didn't have the courage.'

The evening ended on this awkward note and I came away wondering if Spirit had made a mistake this time. But six weeks later she telephoned me. She wanted to come and see me to talk about her feelings. In the course of the conversation she brought up the evening when, through me, the spirits had told her a few home truths.

'I went home in quite a turmoil and sat for hours, not just that night, but for days afterwards. I wondered how I must really look to other people and I didn't like what I saw. What really stuck in my throat was the thought that my daughter and my ex-husband have been so patient and understanding with me all these years.'

She went on to talk about her ex-husband and the man she had been seeing since her divorce. 'He's always been content with our arrangement. I saw him whenever it suited me and we'd always go where I wanted to go. Then I began to wonder why he never brought up the subject of marriage. Of course now I know why. You can imagine my surprise when he proposed to me recently. What do you think I should do, now you know me so well?'

I don't see my role as telling others how to lead their lives so I hesitated to give an answer. My spirit helpers were listening though and they spoke to her again: 'You would be unwise to get married unless you are prepared to change. A leopard *can* change its spots. It's never too late, as long as you realize that you weren't a very nice person before we spoke to you.'

Again I trusted what the spirits had to say. They knew she would appreciate straight talking. It was the only way to give that particular leopard the opportunity to change her spots. But this was only possible because she had reached the point in her life when she was ready to make that change.

As I have already said, I don't think I could learn everything I need to learn on the earth plane in one visit. It seems quite logical to me, therefore, that I have probably been here many times. My spirit guides and helpers certainly have.

Reincarnation is part of the belief system of many Eastern religions and is accepted as a fact by most Spiritualists. When I delved into the subject I discovered that it was also part of the tradition of mystical Judaism.* And many

---

* See *Unto the Churches*, Richard Drummond, Virginia Beach, USA, 1978.

early Christians believed in reincarnation too. Documents discovered in recent years at Nag Hammadi in Egypt and elsewhere, for example, show that it was part of the understanding of many sects, including the Gnostics. It ceased to be an official Christian belief after the Fifth Ecumenical Council of Constantinople in 553 AD when the Bible and other documents were 'adjusted' to bring them into line with the newly formulated doctrine. Even so, the more subtle references have remained intact. John's Gospel (Chapter 9, verses 1-3), for instance, shows both a knowledge of the law of cause and effect and of reincarnation for the purposes of Spirit's progression:

And as Jesus passed by, he saw a man which was blind from his birth. And his disciples asked him, saying, Master, who did sin, this man, or his parents, that he was born blind? Jesus answered, Neither hath this man sinned, nor his parents: but that the works of God should be made manifest in him.

During the course of my healing work I have met people who have had as many as twenty incarnations here. And the well-documented work by Edgar Cayce, and more recently by regression therapists, endorses my own findings. I would therefore say that I do not *believe* in reincarnation, I *know* it to be the case (see also Chapter Six).

I don't know of any instances where human beings have come back as animals or plants or whatever. Spirit has assured me that all forms of Spirit are on separate paths of progression so that humans can only reincarnate as humans.

Sometimes the challenges people have set themselves appear to be too great and they feel unable to face up to them. They become pressurized to the point where they feel they cannot cope any longer. Such people are unaware of their potential, the unique task they chose and the help that is available to them to carry it out. Without this knowledge they may even feel suicidal.

But this is the testing time. It is not until we are tested

by circumstances that we realise our ability to cope with them. Instead of seeing them as a threat we should see them as the thrust block which gives us the chance to gain in strength. But this is not easy for the person who is feeling depressed. First they need the benefit of counselling and healing so that they can face up to this challenge.

People have asked me what to do about friends who are suicidal. I always feel that this is an opportunity to offer the hand of friendship and caring. I advise them to look for the reasons for that person wanting to commit suicide and to try to help them understand their true position. If they can ease them away from the view that life is untenable and help them to cope with the situation, so much the better. But very often the desperate person is in such a confused state that this is impossible. Here the love of other people can help. We tend to stand back when we see a person in such a state, but it is much better to show them that they are loved, that there is a need for them to live and get over things.

This is where judgement needs to be suspended. Let them talk it out of their system, no matter how long it takes. I have listened on the telephone for up to six hours, knowing that I couldn't hang up until the healing power of listening had taken effect.

When I am face to face with the would-be suicide, they become a patient, someone who needs healing. I ask Spirit to go to work just as I would do with a physical problem. A person only contemplates suicide when their life is out of line with their spiritual path. Mental torment indicates that something is desperately wrong; the patient has been confronted with an obstacle which seems insurmountable. Yet, I tell them, they do in fact possess all the resources they need to overcome it. If they end their life, they will not be free from the memory of the situation, but will take it with them in every detail. It may be a source of greater regret to find, on passing over, that nothing has been resolved for they didn't achieve what they set out to and have now lost the opportunity to do so.

These may be tough words, which not all those in desperate straits could take, but Spirit will tell them this if it is appropriate. In any event, my role as a healer is to create an environment of relaxation, love and caring, just as when I am defusing a situation of violence or frustration. For the suicide is angry and frustrated and will go to the extreme of inflicting the ultimate violence on themselves.

I have found that by giving them time to relax and feel reassured, to let them talk and talk, very often they are led to see the way out of the darkness which surrounds them. It is rare that I need to tell anybody what to do, they find it out for themselves because deep down they know.

As I see the depression lifting, I don't encourage them to go until they are ready. By then they are usually glad they came. This is just the first step in the healing process. Most depressed patients need to see me again a number of times and this allows Spirit to continue working on them until things are finally resolved.

Mental pain is just as terrible as physical pain and in many cases a patient's suffering may be quite horrific. My role as healer is to alleviate that suffering so the patient can reconstruct themselves and allow the energy of love to flow through them again.

Our purpose in living is to express fully the God force within us. We don't always make the best of our opportunities because we don't know what tremendous potential we have and how to use it. In the past this knowledge, which is the truth about our real selves, has been withheld from people by those who wanted to control them, such as religious and political leaders. This has left us with a legacy of ignorance, fear and superstition. But we are living at the beginning of the New Age, in a time when awareness of the truth is increasing and can no longer be kept from us.

Even though we use our physical body to travel on this earth plane, we are not confined to it. We can travel anywhere in our etheric body, just as we do in the sleep state. The mind and spirit are free, so we are only restricted if we want to be. We are Spirit. We can be everything and anything.

Our purpose – to fully express the God force – is also the

purpose of the mineral, plant and animal kingdoms. We are here together for our mutual benefit. No one group has precedence over another, for all are Spirit and Spirit is everywhere. This planet, too, is Spirit on a journey of evolution. There is nowhere quite like it in the universe and it provides Spirit with a precious resource for unique experience. For this reason alone, Spirit will not allow it be be destroyed.

Deep within us is our own survival guide which tells us how to make the most of our unique experience, to enjoy fully this adventure of physical life. It tells us that life is for living. We chose it and we had a good reason for coming here.

TEN

Healthy Living – The Survival Guide

If I could synthesize all the help and advice given to my patients by Spirit through me, I might have compiled a guide to living which would be applicable in all situations.

Patients who come to see me initially for healing quite often realize that the cause of their problem is not the state of their health but something deeper, and they wonder whether I can give them any advice about it. They worry about their diet or what exercise they ought to take, and sometimes the advice they seek covers areas of their lives which I wouldn't have considered were my business at all. They think I may be able to give them the answer they are looking for.

When people want this kind of guidance they are assuming that the answer is to be found outside them. But, as I try to explain, the answer is within them, not within somebody else and certainly not within me. I don't give out diet sheets, exercise plans or anything like that. The proliferation of information on all these subjects shows that people are generally more health-conscious, and are seeking ways of taking better care of themselves. But they will find there is no single answer, and what is right for one person will not necessarily be right for another.

To my way of thinking, they are starting at the wrong point. Spirit heals the person, not the condition. It is the person who needs to be looked at first, not their diet or lifestyle. The root of all health problems or any other problems is a spiritual one. Once people begin to look within for their answers, their habits will change naturally and they won't have to impose any regime on themselves. Imposing a regime may help, but it won't bring about the inner changes that are needed. The best regime is the one we work out for ourselves.

There are times when we need to tap the ultimate source of knowledge and wisdom. But having said this, people are not often aware of their own potential and they might need to approach someone, such as a healer, who can tap their source of energy for them to help them find the true answer to their problem. Spirit has shown me that to each person's problem there is an answer and for each person the answer is the one which seems right for them.

So some people maybe surprised at first when I suggest a course of action which ensures that they are still in control of their own lives and able to take responsibility for their own wellbeing. It is a programme anyone can use to compile their own survival guide and it consists of two essential and interdependent processes. These are the processes of looking in at ourselves and of looking out towards others and the environment.

As I mentioned in the previous chapter, we chose to come here for a purpose and that purpose is known to the God force within. Each of us chooses a personality to operate through to achieve our purpose and this is determined by the experience and level of development we bring with us, the characteristics we inherit from our parents and the environment we are born into. So our survival guide needs to be designed to help this personality keep to the pathway leading to our aim or purpose.

It would be true to say that we already have a survival guide. After all, we have survived so far in some way or other so it follows that we must have worked out a strategy for survival. If this has enabled us to get through life so far without any mental, emotional or physical problems we are probably quite happy as we are.

For some, their survival guide is exactly that, a manual for their own personal survival, no matter what the consequences. It does not include attitudes to other people or their treatment of them. It does not include attitudes to the environment and the planet and what is being done to it by their fellow humans. They exclude such matters because they have convinced themselves that they as individuals cannot change or are not interested in changing the state of affairs. Such a survival guide based exclusively on self is patently incomplete since personal survival can be seen to depend more and more on how the planet is faring and on how other people are faring, no matter in what part of the global village they may live. The behaviour of every individual affects all of us whether we like it or not.

From the moment of birth we have tried to work out ways of coping with what has been happening both within us and outside us, and our reactions to these events. This has influenced the formation of the person we see as ourselves and the person we project to others. We have in effect constructed a persona or two personae which may or may not be one and the same, and we attempt to live with and through them to the best of our ability. For some these changes are unconscious, as control is given up to the negative influences around them. But for most of us, changes in personality are conscious and therefore within our control.

Problems begin when we realize that neither the person we see nor the one that others see is really us. Furthermore, for some people one is in conflict with the other. In order to cope we devise further strategies to avoid confronting these conflicts. And these strategies in turn form the mask-like front we present to the world. For many of my patients this has affected not just their physical appearance but their total behaviour. More often than not these strategies are the sign of a sensitive person. I know I needed a mask or a protective shell from quite a young age to cope with my own sensitivity.

Once the personality is out of alignment with our true self, there may be other warning signs such as stress, crisis, illness or other problems. We have to recognize that these warning signs are there for a good reason. They are telling us that somewhere along the line, when we were in the process of compiling our guide, we got it wrong or just missed out something vital. They are urging us to get realigned, to get back on course and live the life we came here to live. When we acknowledge these alarm signals, our higher self or guardian angel can nudge us into taking appropriate action. If this brings a patient to seek help from someone like myself, Spirit can direct the love force into their life and part of the healing process will be to show them how to reconstruct their own survival guide.

The first phase in restoring balance and harmony is to look inwards at ourselves. This will enable us to discover the survival laws which have been disregarded, bringing a breakdown in physical or mental health, or both, and a blocking of the flow of healing energy. There are stages of development in the process and we are not all at the same stage of development. This is why some need healing more than others. If we are out of alignment in this first phase, we cannot be fully effective in our dealings with the outside world, so we have to begin with ourselves.

When we love ourselves, others can learn to love themselves because what we feel rubs off on them. It is an effect of the energy we are projecting. But people who dislike themselves, who are lacking in confidence or feel some sort of inferiority, are ill at ease and dis-ease leads to sickness. Other people are repelled by their negative vibrations and may even feel enmity towards them. On the other hand, people who are at one with themselves feel totally at ease and radiate love energy, confidence and security. In any crowd such a person is easily identifiable, as is the positive effect which they have on those around them. These are the benefits we can bring to ourselves and others through such a positive attitude.

A person may challenge me about this and say: 'That's all very well, Dennis, but we are told to love God above ourselves.' My response is that God is within them and it is for them to love the God within them, not to love from afar, but to love from as close as possible. There is nothing closer than the God force within. This means that we must seriously examine our feelings about ourselves, for they are really our feelings about God.

The body and mind are the instruments we use to express our personality. They both need the right food, the right exercise and the right rest. Loving ourselves means that nothing but the best will do, so we go to our true self to find out the real needs of our body and mind. Of course what is best for one person may not be best for another. Discovering this 'best' means listening and making time to hear the 'still small voice'.

The easiest way to do this is through meditation, which can begin by sitting comfortably and allowing the body and mind to relax. A good way to settle the mind is to day-dream since it can be difficult to empty it completely. When I used to run development circles I used a handful of words which each member could take out of a box. The words would include concepts such as peace, harmony, tranquillity, waterfall, seashore, garden, etc. The idea was to relax and daydream about the word. Gradually, as they got deeper into their picture, they found that they had opened the doorway to their inner temple and they would have different experiences every time. I would open with a prayer asking for protection, to keep the exercise at a spiritual level, then after listening to everyone's description of their meditation, I would close with a prayer of thanks and the hope that we could use the inspiration and peace we had experienced in our daily lives.

The effect of meditation is to change the wavelengths of the brain to what is known as the alpha rhythm and there are other beneficial metabolic changes such as the slowing down of heartbeat and respiration. In this meditative state we can tune in to the inner self which gives access to un-limited energy and so unlimited possibilities. At this level the subconscious mind can be contacted so that subcon-scious knowledge and abilities can be revealed and ex-pressed. Scientists say we utilize only a limited proportion of the brain; this is because our capacities are greater than they have so far discovered. If the brain is 'tuned in', prac-tice will enable the whole of it to be used.

By making the most of meditation we can realize our full

potential as human beings and we can use this capability to set about compiling our survival guide. The inner self knows what we need to eat and drink, how to exercise and rest, and what may be out of balance in any of these areas. We can look at the mind in the same way. If we are not happy with the way we feed it, exercise and rest it, balance can be restored by listening carefully to the promptings of our true self.

As we implement the necessary changes, there is a fool-proof way of checking our progress, for once a state of harmony is allowed to flow into and through us, the body is able to react positively and heal itself. We become healthier, more active, and more resistant to disease. The mind becomes more positive and we can use our own will more easily to counter negative thoughts and influences, whether these originate from within or from without. The more this energy of harmony is able to flow unobstructed, the easier becomes the two-way communication between our outer personality and our inner spirit.

So the essential process of looking in is an active one of seeking alignment with the God force on every front. As soon as we begin we become aware of the power of the mind. It is reluctant to give up old habits, and it may be quite resistant to the promptings of our higher self. This is when we need to remember that the mind is our instrument and we can control it and train it with our will. The power of thought should never be underestimated and the sooner people realize that it is a very powerful form of energy the better. As such, it attracts other energy forms which are like itself and it is this law of attraction that we can use to our advantage in the realignment process. Positive, optimistic, constructive thoughts attract more of the same to us. Sometimes these energy forms will be things, events or encounters with others.

We have the power to change our own state and not let others change it for us. We need to be realistic about the power of other people's negativity and protect ourselves from its effects. This can be done simply by a direct prayer asking for this protection and we can rest assured that we will get it. But we are also evolving beings who sooner or later will have to learn to take responsibility for ourselves. We can begin by closing down after all spiritual activities, as I explained earlier. We can enclose ourselves with a bubble or energy field of light, either by seeing it mentally or by drawing the light from above the head, down the body, under the feet, and up the other side to join over the head, as the breath is inhaled and slowly exhaled.

As a preparation for the important state of sleep, we can clear the mind and body of any negative vibrations which might have been absorbed during the day by drawing pure light into the crown of the head, letting it totally suffuse the body and drain out of the hands and feet with the exhalation of the breath. In the sleep state the brain goes into the meditative wavelength again and it is during this time that we contact the spiritual levels and communicate with the God force. Obviously, the less 'food' is being processed by the mind and body, the easier it will be for them to relax and let this happen. So it is best not to eat too much too late and to let go of anxieties and problems by handing them over in prayer, knowing they will be dealt with by higher forces.

Further opportunities are provided in the sleep state by astral travelling. This is when we use our etheric body to travel, whether on the spiritual levels or the earth plane.* This is quite a natural and regular practice for most of us. If we want to have full recollection of the experience it is simply a matter of training ourselves by thinking before we go to sleep: 'I am going astral travelling and I want to remember where I have been and what I have done.' Eventually we will start to have recall and be able to blend the knowledge of our experiences into our daily lives here.

Having begun the process of harmonizing the inner aspect of the personality, we can start the second essential process which is looking out towards others and the environment. Here we examine our ability to project the flow of

---

* See reference to Maurice Flook in Chapter Seven.

love from ourselves out towards other people, towards animal and plant life, towards our environment and ultimately towards the planet and beyond. Implicit in this second phase are the laws for the community, for the safety of the global village. Just as a disregard for our inner laws brings personal breakdown, so a disregard for these outer laws brings breakdown in the form of social crisis and ecological disaster.

The values of modern society mean that we tend to devote very little time and energy to looking within, but a great deal to the world outside ourselves. Our effect on the external world has therefore been out of alignment with our true selves; and our ravaging and pollution of the planet is an ever-present reminder of this. I know a number of people who are keen campaigners on political and religious issues but whose personal lives are a mess. They have convinced themselves that this has no bearing on their public lives because they keep the two separate. So I ask them why they think they have come to me for help; what is it that has turned them into patients? Some may dismiss the idea of any link, but it sets others thinking and looking more closely at themselves.

The harmonized personality is able to project the flow of harmony outwards and this will show as a caring attitude and a desire to share the energy of love with others. It brings a recognition of being part of a whole since we are automatically linking with the God force without – the God force in other people, in animals and plants and minerals. It emphasizes our inbuilt responsibility as caretakers for all the other forms of Spirit and the importance of knowing what kind of energy we are directing towards them. When we find that any of our attitudes are out of balance, we can go straight to the source of harmony through our contact with the God force within.

Once we have begun to harmonize the outer aspect of the personality we are ready to send healing energy to wherever we see the need. This may be to people in trouble or sickness, animals who are suffering, a devastated landscape, a war-torn city, and so on. Thoughts of love, sympathy, reconciliation, peace and healing are energies which each have their own colour. But we don't need to know what colour these energies are in order to utilize them. When we think of a person or place we send energy to them or into that situation. The more we can relax and allow ourselves to be a channel, the more these unlimited energies can pour out from the God force within to repair whatever is damaged.

So we find that our survival guide helps us to realign both aspects of the personality with the true self and finally to balance them into a harmonious whole. If we are balanced in this way, we stop being 'Jekyll-and-Hyde' characters and there is no conflict between the person inside and the person we project towards the outside.

For some, these two essential processes are consecutive, for others they are concurrent, depending on their level of development. This form of positive evaluation allows us to become channels for the flow of love from its source, so that we can relax and live the life we were meant to live. The whole point of the survival guide is not to make us destructively self-critical and aware of nothing but our shortcomings, for this is a negative approach. Rather, we build on our greatest asset which is that each of us is the God force within.

ELEVEN

Happy, Happy, Happy!

'Bye, Dad, look after yourself.'

I was shaking hands with my son, Mike. There was a sound behind me and I turned and winked at my grandson. He had contracted meningitis in infancy which had left him spastic, epileptic and mentally retarded. He looked at me with bright eyes.

That day was early in 1988. He was eight then and could only utter a few simple words. He flapped his arms about and grinned at me. The thought crossed my mind that, for those who were able to see, nothing could stop his lovely personality from shining through. Had he flapped his 'wings' to tell me that he understood I would soon be up in a plane bound for India?

'Don't you worry, Nicky,' I said to myself. 'I'm going to tell Sai Baba all about you.'

When I am working as a medium in the churches, I find that my spirit helpers like to use a theme to link the talk, the prayers and the clairvoyance. One of the recurrent themes I have been talking about for the past fifteen years has been the coming of the Aquarian age and the probability of a new messiah or avatar. I have sometimes been impressed to use Levi's Aquarian Gospel which describes the Piscean age as being the age of things below the sea and below the earth and the Aquarian age as the age of things above the earth, a time when the human mind will become liberated from its earthbound confinement.

The Aquarian age dawned in August 1987 and one of its

fundamental characteristics is that it is a humanitarian era of caring for all and sharing with all. A growing awareness of the spiritual realities of life is bringing a deeper awareness of each other and all forms of Spirit. We are living in the difficult transition time when new impulses and ideas are gathering strength and making themselves felt, while the old order struggles to resist the inevitable.

I could see many signs of these changes and realized they had touched my consciousness twenty years before when I began healing. I dismissed them then as unrealistic, but events have accelerated since. If there were signs all around me of the New Age coming in, it followed that the avatar must also be here. I would find myself telling congregations that the new messiah was around and we would be hearing of him soon. Afterwards I would wonder why I was saying this when I had no proof of it and nothing to back it up with. The spirits have never let me down so I trusted their reasons for wanting me to speak about it. Then I was told that one day I would go to India and meet the man who had the message I had been looking for.

About five years ago I began to hear of someone called Sai Baba. He was an Indian saint with a mission to save humanity. Though sceptical about such claims I was fired with enthusiasm when the chance came to hear a talk by someone who had been over to India to see him. His main impression seemed to be that Sai Baba could produce little presents for people out of thin air by waving his hands about. They usually took the form of trinkets like rings and bangles. I sat there thinking: 'Well, if that's what you want, you're welcome to it. There are magicians every week on television. I certainly don't need to go all the way to India to see conjuring tricks.' I felt let down. It sounded like so many other stories of Indian gurus told by their over-enthusiastic followers and I dismissed it. Such a person couldn't be the avatar of the New Age. My search would have to continue.

Meanwhile Spirit persisted in speaking about the expected avatar, which made me wonder what sort of person he would be. I pondered on the enormity of his task.

When I considered the state of the planet and the global scale of disruption it seemed something that only one of divine stature could possibly tackle. He would have to be a catalyst powerful enough to stimulate each and every one of us to realign the two aspects of personality with the God force within, while he held the outside world together in the meantime. The ultimate aim would be a global harmonization from which no form of Spirit could be excluded. He would have to be, I decided, the very embodiment of the survival guide.

Strangely, although I had dismissed Sai Baba, I kept hearing the name.

Towards the end of the summer of 1987, I met someone who had investigated Sai Baba more thoroughly. He showed me some books about him and they touched on many things which I thought were more important than the materialization of trinkets. A constant theme was that Sai Baba was a divine incarnation who knew how to use the power of love to bring about the spiritual transformation of the earth. He had come to raise human consciousness and lead us into the New Age.

When I looked at the photographs I was startled to find myself recalling something that had been happening off and on for a number of years. Clairvoyants in church congregations had been coming up to me after my services to say that a little man had been with me. He had a big shock of hair and was dressed in a yellow or orange robe, as the case may be. At the time I had taken such things with a pinch of salt, but the photographs of Sai Baba fitted their descriptions exactly.

My appetite had been whetted and I began to wonder if he really was the person I had been talking about and waiting for.

Through just answering the telephone and saying yes, I have met some very interesting people, many of whom are well known or prominent in their professions. This does not influence my approach to them as patients, but I am grateful for the way Spirit has brought such enrichment into my life. In September 1987 a couple came down from London to have treatment for some quite ordinary conditions. In the course of the conversation afterwards we touched on the subject of Sai Baba and they revealed that they were active in the Sai Baba movement. This was my first meeting with Lucas and Jean Ralli.

On their return to London they sent me some information which included two books about Sai Baba which Lucas had written. Within a few weeks they came to see me again and our conversation about Baba continued. Lucas showed me a picture of the Master Jesus holding a lamb. It was painted on a skeletal leaf and was in a glass-fronted frame, the leaf being about six inches long and four and a half inches wide. Lucas explained the extraordinary story surrounding it.

He got up early one morning and went to work in his study before breakfast, as usual. He had been working at his desk for an hour or so when he decided he would stop for a cup of coffee. When he returned from the kitchen the leaf was resting on top of his papers. The only person in the house beside himself was his wife who was asleep in the bedroom.

Lucas is able to communicate with Sai Baba on a mental level and at the next opportunity he asked if the leaf was from him.

Baba said: 'Yes.'

Lucas told Baba that he had put the leaf in a frame and asked if that was all right.

Baba replied: 'Frame does not matter, the picture matters. Put it where people can see it. Don't put it away.'*

Lucas went on to say that the leaf came from a tree which can only be found in certain parts of India. I guessed it must be growing in Sai Baba's *ashram* (a Sanskrit word meaning 'a spiritual community'). I suppose it was

---

* The leaf is what is known as an *apport*. This is something which materializes somewhere without apparently having been manufactured or brought there. The spirits quite often materialize apports as a gift in order to show their love for someone. A photograph of the leaf appears in *Sai Messages For You and Me, Volume II* by Lucas Ralli.

the leaf that clinched it. While Lucas was telling the story I had made a decision: I would have to go to India to see Sai Baba for myself.

The state of my finances meant that I had no way of doing it, but I found myself saying: 'Well, I've made my mind up. I'm going over to see him. I don't know how and I don't know when, but I'm going.'

Before they left, Lucas said they would keep me in touch with any new developments and I was welcome to attend any of the London events.

The next day the phone rang. It was Jean Ralli. 'If you want to go to India, Dennis, there's a vacancy on the next trip. Don't worry about your expenses. The flight leaves at the end of next January. Would you like to go?'

Without hesitation I said: 'Yes please!'

Aime and Sandra Levy take groups over to India twice a year in February and November. I went up to their home in Kenton to meet them and the other members of the group. They gave us information about the trip and all the jabs we would need and we were advised to have a health check.

My doctor expressed surprise at this latest trip of mine. 'This is your first trip to India, Mr Barrett? It should be quite an experience. And a very long and strenuous journey. Of course you've been to the States a few times so you're used to that side of it. Even so, a total change of climate . . . culture . . . food. Don't take any chances with the water, by the way. I'll have to give you a thorough check-up in view of your medical history.'

I was wondering if there would be any signs of my heart attacks, but he pronounced me in good health and said he would be interested to hear how I got on. He wanted to make sure I was covered for every eventuality so he kitted me out like a chemist's shop. I had pills for constipation and pills for diarrhoea, dehydration capsules, water tablets, sprays and ointments.

The trip had been paid for and I was one hundred per cent fit. My adventure was meant to be. As the day of departure drew nearer, it was with mounting excitement that I went over the things I would need to take with me. I would stay at my son Mike's home in Surrey, as he had offered to drive me up to Heathrow.

The night before the flight I slept well until the early hours of the morning. I like this time of peace and quiet and it is when I get most of my inspiration from Spirit. It was too dark for the birds to be singing, but I could hear a little creature scrabbling about in the flower bed below. Spirit came through and told me the journey I was about to undertake was going to be worthwhile. As a result of going, more things would open up for me than I had ever dreamed possible. This was the beginning of a new chapter in my life.

I met up with the group in the departure lounge at Heathrow. Aime Levy gathered us all together for some last-minute instructions. We would be sitting as a group on the plane, but we would probably have to split up when we took taxis in India so he wanted a man assigned to each smaller group of women. I found myself with Francesca, an Italian; and Val, who had visited Baba before. I asked her what she thought it would be like and she said it was best to go with an open mind because every time was unique and unpredictable and each person experienced it in a different way. Aime said he wanted to tell us his own personal reasons for going to India and finished off with a sincere prayer on behalf of the group. I needed to hear what Aime had to say because it made me realize that Baba hadn't come to found a new religion but to encourage people to do their best in whatever setting they already found themselves. It was a relief to know that I could keep my own identity.

I asked the woman at the check-in if I could have a seat near an aisle with plenty of leg room. This put me alongside an Indian and his family who spent the whole flight to Bombay telling me about Sai Baba and how he had already incarnated before under the name of Sirdi. He gave me a picture of this incarnation and asked me to keep it in a 'holy place'. He also told me if I wanted to avoid being bitten by mosquitoes to get some sandalwood oil and Bangalore was the place to get it. The eight-hour flight soon passed beside my interesting travelling companion and I rejoined the group to pile into a charabanc bound for the domestic airport. While we were loading up I noticed the beggars. Some were really quite jovial while others were too horrifying to look at.

We spent the night in the departure lounge and caught a flight south to Bangalore in the early hours of Monday morning. It was the first day of February. That afternoon I went out with Val and Francesca to explore the city. We found an obliging taxi driver, told him what we wanted to buy, and he knew exactly where to get it. I soon made friends with him and he promised to take us to a restaurant where his countrymen would go. He went in, checked that everything we wanted was available, told the waiters what we wanted and made sure they understood us. Then he waited outside while we had a slap-up meal. Back at the hotel we worked out our expenses and found that the evening, including the meal and taxi, had only cost us fifty rupees each.

It was Tuesday morning and time to set off in the air-conditioned coach to Puttaparthi, the village where Baba was born. We drove through what seemed like a desert. The heat was intense and I was grateful when we stopped at a village for a drink. After three hours in the coach we could see a huge decorated archway ahead of us. The driver stopped and announced with dramatic emphasis: 'We are now approaching the gateway to Baba's kingdom!'

It was an exciting moment, but it was another half hour before we passed through Sai Baba's home village. Finally the coach stopped at the gates to the ashram known as Prasanthi Nilayam. We drove into what seemed like the main street of a village, past rows of office buildings and a large canteen. Finally we drew up by an area of brushed sand and were shown to our dormitories. Men and women live separately in the ashram and even married couples have a job to get permission to stay together.

We just had time to freshen up before going down to the temple for the *darshan* ('audience' or viewing'). The men dressed in pyjama suits and the women had to cover their shoulders and necks. Outside the temple was a vast sandy courtyard with a wide verandah area where everybody formed their lines. We queued up and sat down on the sand. Everything was very orderly and nobody tried to push or take advantage. The lines were headed by ushers who were members of the ashram staff. They guided us to our places and squeezed us all in as tightly as they could. Nobody was allowed to bring in cameras or video equipment; there was no point because apparently nothing would work unless Baba willed it. His aura is so powerful and stretches so far that it interferes with everything electrical. There seemed to be no security apart from a gentle control and general acceptance of the orderly routine.

Thousands of us sat there in silence. This was obligatory for if we had all talked or made a noise the sound would have been deafening. I had seen videos of the darshan, but I still couldn't have anticipated the reality of actually being there. The silence heightened the air of expectancy. I had forgotten the pain in my crossed legs and tried only to remain calm. I could feel my heart beating excitedly. This was the moment I had come all this way for – I was about to see the person whom Lucas Ralli and many other writers referred to as the avatar of the New Age. I was going to have the chance to see him at close quarters and assess these claims for myself.

Then, without anyone saying or doing anything, the silence became even more tangible as our attention was drawn to one corner of the temple courtyard. Sai Baba had appeared. He was a small man in a glowing saffron-coloured robe. An aura of light extended from above his bushy hair to the bottom of his robe. As he came forward he seemed to glide over the ground, to flow rather than walk. His presence immediately filled the enormous space of the courtyard and I could feel the power of the energy that was emanating from him even at a distance of several hundred yards. He went to the women's side first and stopped to talk to some and give out *vibhuti* (sacred ash, materialized by Sai Baba and considered to have beneficial properties, including healing); he sprinkled the ash from his fingertips. When he got to the dividing aisle between the men and the women, the female attendant stepped back and a man stepped forward to escort him.

As he went round like this, he also accepted letters from people, but he was selective and didn't take them all. He made his way down the lines of men and I could feel him getting nearer. Waves of energy seemed to flow before him. These became a total feeling of warmth and peace which filled my heart, then my mind, blotting out all thought. He stopped by me and asked for my letters. His voice was gentle and melodious. I looked up into his eyes and was immediately immersed in an overwhelming love. In that instant he had seen into the depths of my soul and knew me through and through. His glance seemed to encompass every moment of my life and beyond. I struggled to control my emotions and fumbled for the letters which I had tucked inside my shirt. In my own letter I had mentioned all the people who were dear to me and those of my patients with exceptional needs. I also mentioned my grandson, Nicky.

Apparently I was fortunate in being singled out so early in my visit. There were people who had been waiting months for their letter to be taken by Baba. But it was the sight of him that was most important to them. To have the privilege of just seeing a holy person is considered by Indians to be a great blessing in itself.

I sat, still shaken by the experience of Baba's gaze and half watched as he continued to pass in among the rows of men. Although they were sitting so close together, he remained smiling and at ease. The darshan took about half an hour during which Baba walked around the whole area of several thousand people. Besides talking to them and asking where they came from, he also said to some: 'You can go in'. This meant that they could go up and wait on the verandah to have a private audience afterwards.

At noon on the second day I could hear him giving a talk in my mind. I felt sure I would see him that day so it was no surprise when, at the afternoon darshan, the whole of our group of forty were asked to go in. We were ushered into a little reception room. Baba came in, switched on the fan and sat on a throne-like chair in one corner, putting his feet on the footrest. Then he began to talk to us. He was jolly, happy-go-lucky and cheerful, with a gentle and humorous way of putting over his philosophy. He talked about love, devotion, dedication, the God within and our conscience and I found him echoing the words I had heard earlier in my mind and repeating things which Spirit had said through me in the past.

He produced vibhuti and gave some to several of the women. Then he began to joke with us. He asked a young man his name.

'Craig, Swami.' (*Swami* means 'master' or 'teacher' in Sanskrit.)

'No, that is the name of your body. You have no name!' Seeing the surprise on Craig's face, he continued: 'You are Universal Love, you are God. I am God. We are God . . .' He paused and smiled. 'Where are you from?'

We all laughed when Craig replied: 'From you, Swami.'

Baba came close to him and embraced him. 'Now where are you?'

'I am in you, Swami.'

This reply delighted him and he discoursed on the theme 'I am in you, you are in me.' The happy atmosphere seemed to flow around us and into us. In his quiet, relaxed voice he was able to direct his words to everybody in a form which was best suited to their personal needs. We discovered this when we met together in the evening to make a tape recording about what we had experienced during Baba's interviews. We found that each one of us had received a different message.

Each day began at four in the morning with the chanting of OM* in the temple. Although it was cold at this time, hundreds of devotees, both foreign and Indian, would march three times round the temple before entering it. Some of them were going at such a speed I wondered if there was a bonus for making an extra lap! We sat

---

* The sacred Sanskrit syllable said to contain all other sounds; the essence of God in the form of sound.

down inside and the service began with the singing of devotional songs. After this we had just settled ourselves for meditation when the temple bell was banged vigorously above us. I felt as if the brains had been shaken out of my head.

At seven it was time for the first darshan in the courtyard. It took me several days to recover from the strain of sitting cross-legged for just thirty minutes and I was forced to ask for a chair after that, joining the invalids and disabled.

Although it was over 40°C, I wasn't bothered by the heat, and when we rested in the early afternoon I just lay in a pool of sweat. I enjoyed the food and found that unlike many members of the group I didn't suffer from any digestive problems. Several of them asked for healing for diarrhoea and all the medicines my doctor had prescribed for me came in handy for other people at some time during the three weeks of our stay.

One afternoon I decided to explore the ashram. Most of the buildings were painted in pastel shades of blue, pink and cream which enhanced the peaceful atmosphere. A wall surrounded the ashram and there were attendants at the gateways. The three domes of the temple, capped with gold, could be seen wherever I went. In front of the temple was the great courtyard of brushed sand surrounded by a wall, and inside the wall were a number of porches each decorated with coloured friezes.

Later on I came across a tree with leaves just like the one Lucas Ralli had shown me back in London. It was the only one of its kind in the area. There were trees everywhere in this kingdom of Baba's, yet the countryside around it was almost a desert. Round the courtyard were coconut palms and beautiful luxuriant plants. All this foliage provided a home for a family of large monkeys and thousands of nesting birds. They would fly off at the crack of dawn and were not seen again until nightfall. Throughout the day a variety of other birds flew in and out of the ashram – buzzards, eagles, larks and all kinds of songbirds. I never saw one being attacked and I never saw any bird droppings. It was as if even the birds treated the territory as sacred.

As I wandered around I thought about the vast amount of water needed to supply all the taps and showers but I could see no tanks or waterworks. The only visible source of water was a river bed which had apparently been dry for years. I asked an attendant where the water came from. He smiled and said that Baba blessed the taps! This explanation seemed quite satisfactory to most people since Baba quite evidently *did* cater for everyone's needs.

The following Saturday most of our group were asked to go for another audience, along with some Italians and a group from Cornwall. We were ushered in and as I approached Baba he said: 'Hurry, Question Mark, time is very precious. There's a lot of jealousy out there!'

I took my place in the reception room and sat smiling to myself. So it was true that Baba knew what was in our minds. I was very sceptical about the stories of his divine nature and, by calling me 'Question Mark', he seemed to be telling me that he knew the purpose of my visit was to check him out.

He spoke again on the subjects he had discussed the previous Wednesday as if to clear up any queries we might have had. Then he produced vibhuti again and handed it round to various members of the group. He sensed that one of the men wanted a watch and began to materialize it. The buckle appeared first, then the strap, then the watch. As it appeared, the watch started to tick. He held his hand out for the watch to finish materializing and drop into it. When he does anything like this, he waves his right hand then holds it up, palm forward. His sleeve drops down nearly to his elbow so there is no way that anything can happen between his sleeve and his hand. Things grow in the air in front of his hand, not out of the palm. They materialize as if being extruded out of a mould.

He looked at the watch that had dropped into his hand and checked the time. Then he said to one of us: 'Your watch is wrong, my watch is right.'

Sure enough it was slow and everyone else's watch agreed with Baba's.

One of the women was wearing several pieces of jewellery. Baba looked at her and asked: 'Do you know what you want?'

'Yes, I do.'

'I'll give it to you.'

He waved his hand and watched intently to see what it was she wanted. I realized then that he didn't materialize these objects to show how clever he was or even to satisfy our need for miracles. He simply wanted to grant everybody's wish. When a bracelet appeared he said: 'Is that what you wanted?'

'Yes, Swami,' she said.

He shrugged his shoulders as if to say: 'Some people are easily satisfied', and put it on her wrist.

One of my friends from Cardiff was sitting with us that day. He is a reflexologist and he has sent a number of his patients to see me. Graham had lost the ring he was using to keep his scarf in place. We were all wearing blue scarves to show that we were members of the London group and we had each been given a ring to act as a toggle. He had bought another one at the shop and was wearing it on his finger. Baba pointed to it and asked: 'What have you got there?'

'A ring, Swami.'

'Why are you wearing that?'

I lost the first one and had to go and get another from the shop so I thought I'd better put it on my finger to make sure I don't lose it.'

'Would you like a ring?'

'Yes, please, I'd love one!'

So Baba began to materialize a ring for him. He held his hand out, caught it and handed it to Graham. He watched him put it on. It fitted perfectly.

'Is that all you want?'

'No, Swami.'

'What else do you want?'

'I want a heart.'

Baba considered this for a moment, then said: 'You shall have it.' He held up his hand and pointed the palm towards him.

Later Graham told us about his unusual request. 'All my life I've been emotionally uptight. I've missed out through not being able to feel anything. But after Swami said I could have a heart I felt it warm up. I went away and cried my eyes out. It was the first time I had been able to let my emotions go. He knew what I wanted and what I needed. He knew I wasn't satisfied with a ring.'

When we came out of the interview I met a Sikh who was in control of the seating arrangements. He wanted to know if Baba had materialized anything. People seemed to be fascinated by this aspect of his personality and I wondered if he used this ability to draw people to hear his message. Later I learned that Baba had once explained:
'For me, a materialization is a kind of visiting card to convince people of my love for them and secure their devotion in return. Since love is formless I use materialization as evidence of my love. It is merely a symbol. Most people desire a talisman symbolic of my protection, so I provide them. These trinkets or talismans give people a sense of security and protection they need in time of trouble or crisis and create a symbolic link covering the long distances between them and myself. When the devotees need me, these objects flash the message as if by wireless and I instantly come to their rescue.'

The next day I was talking to an Indian who published the ashram magazine and I told him I was with the London group. At this his face lit up. 'Baba says the London group ask the right questions and they provide him with an opportunity to give them the answers. He likes the London group because they are interested in philosophy and the reason behind things. They don't just want him for what they can get out of him in the way of presents.'

Sitting in the courtyard among the thousands of pilgrims, I sometimes used to wonder what Baba wanted for himself. One hot afternoon I watched some of the Indians impede his progress as they tried to kiss his feet. I found myself becoming annoyed at this and I wanted them to be more considerate of his wishes.

195

'God bless you,' I thought. 'Why do you let them do it? Why don't you stop them?'

And he looked up from quite a distance away and smiled. As his eyes met mine it was as if there was a silver rod between us. Again, the overwhelming sensations of love and peace flooded into me. I knew that he was instantly aware of both my concern and my irritation. The words came into my mind: 'It's all right. They don't hurt me and it's helping them. Thank you.'

He carried on round the courtyard and came over to the old men's chairs where I was sitting. He looked at me and asked: 'How are you?'

'I'm fine, thank you. How are you?'

He beamed and said: 'I'm *always* fine!'

This was true. He was always fine. He seemed to want nothing for himself except to give out a never-ending stream of love towards everybody. I never saw him lose patience with anyone. I never saw him out of countenance, yet he was said to work twenty-four hours a day. No one had ever seen him asleep, yet he was fit and happy at all times.

His whole life has been remarkable, from the day he was born of humble but very spiritual parents in a simple village house. Perhaps, I wondered, his life couldn't be judged by ordinary standards since so much of it seemed to be shot through with the miraculous. At the age of eight he made different fruits appear on the same barren tree and he continued to astound his family and his playmates in this way. One day, for example, they were at the bottom of a steep hill and Baba challenged them to a race to the top. His friends had hardly taken a step before he appeared the next instant at the top. Such incidents were merely the prelude to a life in which the unbelievable became a daily occurrence.

He was fourteen when he left the village school and told his parents he would not be their child any more for he had to start his work. From then on he began to teach and people came hundreds of miles to hear him. He now has tens of millions of devotees all over the world. He is accepted by heads of state and many of the world's leaders have been to see him. He is responsible for twenty-eight universities, colleges and schools and for the free hospital where anyone may go for treatment. He accepts no money and no one in the ashram will accept either presents or money. People are allowed to make endowments or donations towards the cost of educating the thousands of students, but that is all.

He is also permanently responsible for the accommodaton and wellbeing of several thousand pilgrims and devotees whose constantly changing numbers swell to thousands more at festival time. I was there during Shivaratri, a great Hindu celebration. Coaches had been turning up all through the day before and all night. There was a hall which seated 20,000 people and when we went down at four o'clock it was full up with at least another five thousand outside. Baba addressed the crowd and the various speeches and ceremonials lasted until seven when everybody was provided with a meal. That morning no one had known what was going to be made or how all the people would be fed, but they were. The next day the same thing happened again and there was plenty of food left over. People were told to save this because it had been blessed by Baba. He didn't materialize it, but he organized the cooking and preparation of it.

It was said that he could be in two places at once and was seen performing an operation in a hospital while he was also present somewhere else at the same moment. On three occasions I saw his attendant casting a shadow while he did not. On one of these occasions he stepped on the foot of one of our group who said she felt no weight or discomfort. He was able to be present in and make visible his astral body while his physical body was somewhere else.

I was satisfied that I had witnessed with my own eyes his capacity to materialize any object out of nothing, without any possibility of sleight of hand. Even so, I don't believe anything until it is proved and I wanted to see the hill which Baba was said to have nipped up in a trice. A number of our group also wanted to visit the hill so we went along there together.

I was surprised to see that it rose very steeply out of the

ground. Girls came up to us selling garlands of flowers. They seemed to be selling them for the sheer fun of it because if you said no, they laughed and gave you one for nothing. There were a good hundred and fifty steep steps carved into the hillside and some of our party wanted to see how quickly they could make it to the top. With my shortness of breath, nothing would have got me up there. When they got back over half an hour later one of the women said she had left her scarf at the top. One of the garland sellers offered to go and get it for her and away she went, running up the steps. It reminded me of the men who run up and down the pyramids in Egypt for a tip. She ran all the way back down again, but it still took her over ten minutes. I could almost hear a voice inside me asking: 'Are you convinced yet, Dennis?'

Baba is also supposed to be able to control the weather. On a certain festive occasion rain was imminent and there was talk of holding the celebrations indoors. Baba said to stay outdoors in the temple courtyard and the weather was perfect. But once the festivities were over and they went outside the courtyard they found everything swimming in water. It had been raining heavily outside the courtyard but not above it. This seemed a bit of wishful thinking to me and I decided I would need my own proof about this aspect of Baba's abilities.

Even so, I like the story of a certain couple who flew out to India to see him. The husband was quite a sceptic, like me, and during the flight he said to his wife: 'I'd like to see him do something a man *can't* do. That would convince me.' Later on after they had landed, they were passing through the desert on the way to the ashram when they saw a beautiful rainbow. But unlike a normal rainbow this one was a vertical column of light going up from the earth into the sky. There was no rain and there had been no rain in the area for some time. The man was delighted to see this natural phenomenon and so was his wife and they decided it must be something special to that part of the world. When they got to the ashram they were seated in the courtyard waiting for Baba's darshan. He appeared and, out of the thousands of people sitting there, he came and picked out the husband. Bending over him, he asked: 'Well, can man produce a rainbow?'

He has often been asked why he does not stop all the disaster and misery in the world. His reply is that he could stop all of it as simply as snapping his fingers, but, if he did this, in two weeks things would be just the same as before because humanity wouldn't have changed from within. People must learn to do it themselves or they will never realize their own divine capabilities. But he will not allow Armageddon to happen; in fact he came here to avert it. In 1987 he said that the next thirty years of his life were going to be the most important to humanity because he would come to be known all over the world. So I am looking forward to seeing whether we will take up his challenge to let the God force within change our lives.

While I was there I met quite a few people who seemed to be making a career out of staying at the ashram. During the first week I was talking to a young man from Cornwall. He had been there nearly six months and at the end of that time he would have to leave the country because his visa would have expired. A visa lasted three months and could be extended for only three more months. I asked him what his plans were after that. He thought for a moment and said: 'I've decided to go to Malaysia for a fortnight. Then I'll apply for another visa and come straight back here.'

Perhaps he thought I would admire his devotion, but I wondered what he had been doing with himself all those months at the ashram.

'Keeping out of the way of Sai Baba,' he said.

'What do you mean by that?'

'Well, I stay at the back of the darshan so that he won't talk to me.'

'Why don't you want him to talk to you? Some people would give their eyeteeth for that.'

'Because if he talks to me he'll probably tell me to go. If he doesn't talk to me he can't tell me to go.'

'And you really believe he doesn't know you're here?'

He shrugged his shoulders.

'Well, I can't see the point in staying if you're not welcome. What are you doing for *him*?'

'Oh,' he said, 'I love him!'

'You love him so much you want to keep out of his sight? That's not my idea of love!'

'Well, let's not tread on each other's corns, Dennis. I'll think about what you've said.'

A week later it was my turn to look after Roy in his wheelchair. When we came out of the hymn-singing, Roy said he had been asked if he would like to go up to the print shop to help put labels on magazines. It was a relief to be able to go somewhere else. The London group had spent the week talking in whispers and, for someone who is hard of hearing as I am, it was proving to be a strain. We were shown to a table on which the work was set out and we sat down. I found myself next to Jim, an American doctor from Illinois who was eager to engage me in conversation. The talk soon got round to Baba and he started to say how much he loved him and what a blessing it was to be near such a wonderful person.

'This is great,' I said. 'How long have you been here?'

'Oh, several months now.'

My first thought was how could he afford to be away from his practice for so long?

'What are you going to do now?' I asked.

'Stay here at the ashram.'

'What for?'

'To be honest with you, Dennis, I just want to be near Baba. I want to hear his teaching.'

'But surely Baba's not giving out his teaching just for you to stay here and waste it? Why don't you go home and start using it?'

'Well, I don't know about that.'

'I do,' I said. 'I can't get home fast enough. I've been here nearly three weeks and, as far as I'm concerned, I've learned all I want to learn.'

'What's the most important thing you've learned, Dennis?'

'I've learned that the inner voice is the one I need to follow and it is the same voice as Baba's. I'm convinced that his message and the one I get from Spirit is the same. I haven't heard anything different over here to what I hear in England. But I *have* met the person who I think is here to proclaim the message to those who can't accept it in any other way than from a personality.'

Jim looked very thoughtful. 'Oh . . . I hadn't seen it like that. So you think I'm opting out, then?'

'I think you're a coward. What's the good of staying here in India and letting Baba do all the work? Get out and work, man. Show the flag!'

Jim looked a bit downcast when Roy and I left the print shop, but I felt it was one of those times when I couldn't sugar the pill. He had asked for my opinion and I had given it. The rest was up to him. It was lovely to hear from him some time later. He had gone back to the States and opened up a healing centre which was doing very well.

William was another young American I met who seemed to be hiding from reality. He was from San Francisco and had been travelling the East searching for an answer to his spiritual dilemmas. He seemed to look on me as a father figure and I was quite happy to take on this role. He had been in Baba's vicinity for many months and wanted to know what I thought about the spiritual side of life. I said I had spent the past twenty years talking to people about such things and if he really wanted to go into it we would have to set aside some time.

'That's fine, Dennis. Perhaps we could go for a walk and talk as we go?'

So we walked out of the village and into the surrounding hills where we found a place to sit down among the rocks. We talked about his spiritual quest and I answered all his questions on life after death, what we are here for, whatever he wanted to hear about. He became more and more enthralled and said he had never heard such things explained before.

I thought: 'What has this fellow been doing over here all this time? The whole story of Baba is the purpose of living.' He spent much of his discourses stressing the benefits of loving service in expanding the heart and making life purposeful. So I asked William what he did with his time in the ashram.

'I read all the books on Baba in the bookstalls. I rest. I attend the darshan. I keep out of sight, though, so Baba won't see me.'

Here was another one keeping his head down. It was a waste of a young man's life, I thought. I steered the conversation to point out, in a positive way, what he was missing by not being involved in living. I realized as I was talking that he might not feel he was missing anything. It was his free choice anyway.

At this point a scorpion came sidling towards us from behind a stone. I had never seen one at such close quarters before, but William was quite calm and ushered it out of the way. 'Don't worry, Dennis, they won't hurt you if you don't hurt them.'

It was as if the scorpion's appearance marked the end of our talk and we set off back to the ashram.

These three young men may not have realized it, but they gave me food for thought too. I found it intriguing that Baba *had* seemingly overlooked them, yet this fact was not telling them anything. I had been prompted to help them realize that they were not solving their problems by staying at Baba's ashram and they were not helping him either by remaining there. In doing so, I was confronting my own queries. I had come over to confirm that he could do everything that I had read about in the books, but I had also wanted my own proof of his divinity. I had been able to speak with conviction about these things. Something was telling me that I knew the answer to my questions and that I had been given the proof I needed.

The day before we were due to leave, Baba invited the London group to 'go in' again for our third audience. The attendant said we were the 'thrice blessed'. Baba was in a jolly mood and joked with us again. He asked my roommate from Blackpool, Allan, what his birthstone was. This surprised us since we had been discussing the subject that very morning and he had found out that his was a diamond. So we laughed when he said: 'A diamond, Swami!'

Baba smiled. 'No diamond, but I have a pretty stone for you. It will bring you a special blessing.'

With that he waved his hand and a ring appeared in front of it. He passed it to Allan who saw that it was set with a beautiful blue stone.

'It's just what I've always wanted, Swami.'

Baba laughed and put it firmly on Allan's finger. 'My rings always fit!'

Several of the women asked him to bless photos of their husbands. One was a widow. Baba took the photo and looked at it. 'He loved you very much.'

'Yes, he did.'

'You argued a lot though. You were naughty!'

This raised a general laugh, then Baba said very gently: 'Don't worry . . . he understands.'

Patsy asked if she was right to use a crystal in her healing. He asked to see it and held it for a moment. 'This is part of the earth. It is in your mind that you can do things, not in the earth. You don't need this.'

I think she expected it to dematerialize for a moment, but he handed it back to her and discoursed on the power of the mind and the divine potential of humanity which we had so far failed to use. This was because we refused to accept the truth which was that we are all God. He was God and so was Patsy's crystal.

One of the women said: 'Swami, you are constantly helping us. How can we help you?'

Baba replied immediately. 'I don't need help. I am Spirit. I am in everything. I am in him, in her, in you.' He pointed to the flowers and objects around us. 'I am in this. I am in that. I am doing day and night. I don't need help. Help yourself first, help others next. Don't help others first.'

He talked on this theme for a few minutes and patiently answered all our questions. Then he turned to the woman who had asked how we could help and pointed to the windowsill. 'Hand me down the carrier.'

She reached out and passed him a carrier bag which contained packets of vibhuti. As he took hold of one handle, he let her hold the other and beamed at her. 'You *can* help me!'

He asked us when we were going home and we said with one voice: 'Tomorrow!'

He laughed and said: 'Tomorrow. Tomorrow. I'm very happy. Happy, happy, happy!'

I thought: 'Why does he repeat himself like that?' It was as if he had heard my thoughts for he drew me back to what he was saying. 'Come again. This is your home. I am yours. You are mine. If you want anything, ask and I will give it to you.'

Patsy said: 'I want to stay, Swami.'

He smiled at her. 'But I am always with you, why do you want to stay here? Go home and love everybody as you do me.' Then he jumped up and said: 'You're hot. I'm hot! Come, we must go.'

He opened the door and went out. I got up and followed the others outside. Something made me turn my head and I saw him standing in the porch of the temple laughing his head off. I nodded to him. He waved back and pointed the palm of his hand at me. I felt the energy from this gesture engulf me and at the same moment came the knowledge, like warmth in my mind and heart – he knew that I knew.

Then, as we stepped out onto the sand of the courtyard, rain fairly fell out of the sky and in moments we were saturated. I looked up and could see no clouds anywhere. Then I looked back towards the temple and Baba was laughing harder than ever. But by the time we reached the edge of the courtyard it had stopped raining.

There had been neither rain nor even clouds during the whole of our three-week stay. In fact the ashram staff had been saying that it hadn't rained for months. I wanted to laugh too. Baba loved a bit of fun. Just when I no longer needed any further proof about him, he had shown me he could control the weather!

The next day I was getting ready to leave and found a letter on my bed from William, the young American. He was going to see the planetarium show and thought he might not be back in time to say goodbye. He wanted to thank me for our conversations together and included a drawing he had made of one of the wild flowers that grew nearby. On it was the inscription: 'Take this hand, this flesh, this instrument and mould for me one gesture, perfect and complete.'

Into my mind flashed a picture of Baba holding the palm of his hand towards me as he stood in the temple, the same hand that gave Graham back his heart.

On the flight home I began to understand what he had given me as I relived all the hundreds of experiences I had been through in such a short time. I knew I had been meant to go because the moment was right and I was ready. I had needed to see for myself and Baba had answered all my questions in so many different ways. I had seen that his life was dedicated to loving people and helping them to love themselves and each other. He had shown me that this unblocked the heart chakra so that love could flow throughout the body and out to all those who passed us by or came to play a part in our lives.

We were up in the clouds now and I imagined I could look down upon the planet earth and see the light which radiated from that little village in southern India. It reached up into the sky to touch the birds and aircraft as they passed overhead. It poured out into the world to impress the hardest heart and help unblock the heart chakra of the planet.

It is said that when human beings have lost their way and life becomes untenable on the earth, God takes the human form of the avatar to relight the lamp of love. Now, when 'the little man in a saffron robe with a big shock of hair' was with me again, I would know who it was. It would be the God force in person.

Mike met me at Heathrow with his eldest son, Matthew, and we drove down to Deepcut together. Soon the English countryside became familiar again. It was good to be back home, but it was almost a shock to absorb the particular greens, the late February light, the trees still in their winter bareness. The tremendous heat and brightness, the special smell of India began to recede in my mind. The dusty road back to Bangalore, the teeming streets of Bombay, the overwhelming atmosphere of peace and love in Baba's ashram hovered like the memory of a vivid dream.

Mike wanted to know how I had enjoyed myself. Matthew wondered what India was like. I looked out of the car window at the hedgerows. There would be no bullock cart round the next bend; no laughing, dark-faced children jumping and shouting by the roadside.

The car drew up outside the house and the front door opened. My daughter-in-law, Marilyn, was there to greet us. As I came in Nicky came charging up the passage. He lurched over and put his arms around me in his own special way. As we hugged each other he cried: 'Happy, happy, happy! Baba, baba, baba!'

My hair stood on end as I recognized the voice. It was the same voice I had heard Baba use and they were the clearest words I had ever heard Nicky speak.

I watched him as we sat down to tea. He was still epileptic, still spastic and still mentally handicapped. But he was in God's hands, he had Baba with him.

The whole experience of Baba had brought a sense of completeness to my life. The avatar of the New Age wasn't wishful thinking but a living reality. I knew that he was on this planet now, in human form, in our lifetime and sooner or later each and every one of us would be affected by this fact. I was ready to go on with this new knowledge, to spread the message that all we have to do is to be true to our real selves, the God force within.

That night I fell asleep with three words ringing in my ears: 'Happy, happy, happy!'